DIESTERWEGS
NEUSPRACHLICHE
BIBLIOTHEK

Joyce Carol Oates

Freaky Green Eyes

Edited and annotated
by
Arthur Kutsch

DIESTERWEG

Published by arrangement with the Harper Collins Childrens Books,
a division of Harper Collins Publishers

Druck A⁴ / Jahr 2016
Alle Drucke der Serie A sind im Unterricht parallel verwendbar.

Umschlagfoto: aboutpixel.de / Party People © Arnim Schindler
Umschlagkonzeption: Blum-Design und Kommunikation, Hamburg
Umschlagrealisation: Harald Thumser, Frankfurt am Main
Satz: Stahringer Satz GmbH, Grünberg
Druck und Bindung: Westermann Druck Zwickau GmbH

ISBN 978-3-425-04853-6

Contents

The Author and her Work

Born in 1938 near the small city of Lockport, New York State, Joyce Carol Oates grew up in the working-class environment of her grandparents' farm in Erie County which she lovingly recalls in many of her novels and stories. After attending high school she studied at Syracuse University, NY from 1956, where she frequently published in the university's literary magazine. In 1960 she received her B.A. degree at the top of her class and then transferred to the University of Wisconsin where she received an M.A. in English in 1961. In the same year she married Raymond Joseph Smith, a fellow English student. In 1962 she was appointed to a teaching position in English at the University of Detroit. The social tensions of this city had a lasting impact on her writing and her first novel, *With Shuddering Fall* (1964), announced her familiar themes of madness, violence and sexual passion.

The decade from 1968 to 1978, when Oates taught at the University of Windsor in Canada, was immensely productive, for she published two or three new books per year, while maintaining her full-time academic career. Finally she accepted a position of professor and writer in residence at Princeton University, NJ. Here she and her husband, who was on the academic staff, too, founded a literary magazine, the *Ontario Review*. Since 1981 she has been a distinguished professor there and today Joyce Carol Oates is one of the most prolific and distinguished writers of the United

States. Meanwhile she has written hundreds of short stories, and more than sixty novels, novellas, young adult and children's fiction—partly under the pseudonyms Rosamond Smith and Lauren Kelly. Moreover, Joyce Carol Oates is a successful playwright, a poet, and the author of a number of critical works, newspaper articles, and last but not least the editor of various anthologies. Her enormous success as a writer is reflected in the great number of prizes she has won. Among them multiple O. Henry Awards and the National Book Award.

Although Oates' fictional work embraces a variety of styles, one can say that two factors are predominant: on the one hand her being rooted in American naturalism and reality and on the other hand her preoccupation with violence.

Her young adult novel *Freaky Green Eyes* (2003) is a symbiosis of the "crime novel" and the "novel proper", for in this psychological thriller J. C. Oates uses typical elements of "escape literature" in order to deliver serious messages. The book was nominated for the German "Jugendliteraturpreis 2006".

Abbreviations

adj.	– adjective
adv.	– adverb
AE	– American English
anat.	– anatomic
bot.	– botanical
BE	– British English
derog.	– derogatory
esp.	– especially
etc.	– et cetera; and so on
fig.	– figurative/metaphorical
fml.	– formal
i.e.	– id est; that is to say; in other words
inf.	– informal
interj.	– interjection, exclamation
lit.	– literary
n	– noun
pl.	– plural
resp.	– respectively
sb.	– somebody
sl.	– slang
sth.	– something
usu.	– usually
vulg.	– vulgar, rude

I

Crossing Over

ONE

how freaky green eyes got her name

Later, I would think of it as crossing over. Maybe it was what my mother was doing, too. Crossing over. From a known territory into an unknown. From a place where people know you to a place where people only think they know you.

Like there's an actual river you swim across, an unpredictable, treacherous river, and if you make it to the farther shore, you're a different person than the one you were when you started out.

It began with me a year ago this past July. A few weeks after my fourteenth birthday. When Freaky Green Eyes came into my heart.

The stuff between my parents hadn't started yet. Well, probably it had but I wasn't picking up signals. Wasn't wanting to.

I hooked up with this older guy at a party, and it was a bad episode or would've been except for Freaky.

Where Freaky emerged from, I don't know. I've never told anyone about this, not even Twyla, who's my closest friend and what you'd call a calming influence on me. I never told Mom, though this was a time when we were still pretty close and I guess I should have told her, looking back on it.

The party was at some rich people's place on Puget Sound north of the city. My family (except for my older brother, Todd, who hadn't come with us) were house guests at the home of neighbors of these people, also very rich with a spectacular house on the Sound. The crowd was entirely made up of people I didn't know, mostly college age. A girl from my school in Seattle, Forrester Academy, invited me along with a bunch of her friends, and when we showed up it was painfully obvious that I was like the youngest individual in the room. With my milky, freckled skin and carroty-red hair pulled back in a ponytail that sort of exploded out in frizz and static electricity halfway down my back, and a scared look, plus

freaky (inf.) strange **unpredictable** incalculable, unforeseeable **treacherous** ['tretʃərəs] here: dangerous **stuff** here: complications, difficulties **to hook up with sb.** to become involved (start an affair) with sb. **guy** (inf.) fellow, type **to emerge from** here: to develop, come into being **Puget Sound** [pju:djid] a very large bay or salt water estuary of the eastern North Pacific with many channels and branches extending from the southern end of Whidbey Island to Olympia, the capital of Washington State **Seattle** the largest city in the state of Washington. Situated between Puget Sound and Lake Washington **bunch** group **freckled** with pale brown spots on the skin **frizz and static electricity** *kraus und elektrostatisch aufgeladen* **to scare** to frighten

the skinny pink tube top and flip-flops, and no makeup, definitely I gave signals of being the youngest.

The girls I'd come with dumped me in record time.

It was a mile at least back to the house my family was staying in, and along a busy shore road with no sidewalks. Still, I wanted to turn and run out of that party the first few seconds I stepped into that scene.

Franky Pierson, climbing to the high board. Poised to dive, then freezing.

Except it was no diving event. I might have been invisible; nobody so much as glanced at me.

The music was so loud, I almost couldn't hear it. Hard heavy-metal rock? Right away my heart began beating fast with this music, the way my heart tends to do in any nerved-up situation. My dad liked to say that though I look like my mom, I take after him: he's a former athlete, a pro football player, and he says we take our cues from the immediate environment, like birds and animals do. If you're challenged, it's FIGHT or FLIGHT.

Definitely, I wasn't in a mood to FIGHT. But FLIGHT didn't appeal to me much either.

After a few minutes it was weird—I began to like the music. I mean, basically I hated the music, but I began to like the nerved-up sensation.

People were jammed into a long living room with glass walls overlooking the Sound. In midsummer the sun sets late in the Pacific Northwest, and it had nearly fallen beneath the horizon now, flamy red streaks on the rippling water, but nobody at this party was paying any attention to the landscape.

I drifted at the edge of the party, trying not to be jostled by strangers with dangerously sloshing drinks. By the smell of the room, it was beer they were drinking. Like flotsam, I was pushed along and found myself in another long glass-walled room, this one even bigger than the other,

tube top AE a shoulderless, sleeveless, tight-fitting garment that covers the upper part of the body, kept in place by elasticity **flip-flops** type of open sandals, *Badelatschen* **to dump sb.** (inf.) to abandon, break up with sb. **poised** ready to act or move **to freeze** to stop dead, become motionless **to tend to do** to be inclined to do **nerved-up** here: tense **pro** (n) (inf.) professional **to take one's cues from sth.** here: to react spontaneously to sth. **to appeal to sb.** attract sb. **weird** [wɪəd] peculiar, bizarre **to be jammed** to be crowded, packed **flamy** fiery red **streak** (n) line, stripe **rippling** moving in a series of small waves **to drift** to wander aimlessly **to slosh** to pour, splash **flotsam** (n) floating remains, wreckage

overlooking a dock with a tall, sleek sailboat and a large yacht moored at it. Everywhere were people I didn't know, good-looking guys, glamorous girls, years older than me and showing lots of skin. It was like a pane of opaque glass was between us: they were in a dimension I couldn't enter. Yet I was stubborn; I didn't run away.

Thinking of my mom, complaining it was a strain on her, being with people most of the time who only want to meet Dad, the local celebrity "Reid Pierson." They almost totally ignored her, she said, or spoke to her in a condescending way. ("Oh, and what do you do?") Mom said she felt as if she didn't exist, and this was the way I was feeling, embarrassed yet excited, too, hopeful. I was glancing around the party with a pathetic little smile of expectation, anticipation—like at any second someone was going to come up and hug me.

Some good-looking guy, a senior from Forrester, pushing through the crowd saying, "Francesca? *Hi.*"

It didn't happen that way. Not quite.

Instead, I located a bathroom, gleaming white tile like pearl, a fancy Jacuzzi with brass fixtures, and in the mirror my flushed-cheeked face, and baffled/hurt/stoic green eyes. I was embarrassed to see myself, but who else did I expect?

It was only about a year since I'd started my period. ("Started my period": what a dumb-ass expression!) I'd been pretty much a tomboy before that; now I didn't know what I was, exactly. A girl, sure. But not a girly-girl.

Or maybe that's what I am. Francesca Pierson, not Franky. And I'm fighting it.

Denial, it's called.

When Mom was my age, she said, she'd been "obsessed" with her looks. And with guys. She told me she'd done some pretty reckless things that might've messed her life up permanently except she was lucky. ("More lucky than smart, Francesca.") So I worried sometimes maybe I resem-

sleek shining, gleaming **to moor** to fasten a ship, anchor **opaque** non transparent **stubborn** (adj.) determined not to give up **celebrity** famous person **condescending** partronizing, snobbish **pathetic** pitiful, miserable **to hug sb.** to embrace sb. **tile** *Wandfliese* **fancy** (adj.) decorative, luxurious **Jacuzzi** a whirlpool bathtub **fixtures** installments, fittings **flushed** red **baffled** bewildered, perplexed **stoic** (adj.) long-suffering **tomboy** a girl fond of rough and noisy activities **girly-girl** (sl.) a girl or woman who likes to dress and behave in a traditional feminine way **denial** refusal, negation **obsessed** to have one's mind filled with an idea so that you can think of nothing else **reckless** rash and wild, careless **to mess sth. up** to throw into disorder

bled my mother more than I wanted to think I did. That I would become "obsessed" with my looks in high school like just about everybody else I know.

"Francesca, *hi.*"

I wink at myself in the mirror. Shake out my ponytail. Decide I look okay. Not glamorous, but okay.

"Hi."

Don't ask me how, or why: a guy appears out of the crowd nudging into me by accident, then decides to pause, and check me out, and smile. I'm grinning back like a lighted Halloween pumpkin. It's perverse how my nerved-up state subsides—I'm playing the role of a girl who isn't excited/scared/thrilled-to bursting. You'd think this was a movie party scene, I'd played this role before.

This guy who's smiling at me, who seems actually to like me, is shouting in my ear that his name is "Cameron"—I can't make out the last name. He's a freshman at USC—I feel really stupid asking what is "USC" (University of Southern California). He asks my name, and I tell him "Francesca"—suddenly Franky sounds juvenile—and I kind of mumble where I go to school. Cameron says that his family lives on Vashon Island in Seattle, his dad is an executive at Boeing, they have a summer place on the Sound, and he's crazy about sailing, and what about me? I can smell the beer on his breath, we're standing so close. Getting jostled by people, which pushes us even closer together. I hear myself tell Cameron, practically shouting into his ear, that my family lives in Yarrow Heights, and we're staying just for a few days with friends on the Sound, not giving details like who my father is, and whose house guests we are, because the name of my father's friend is pretty famous. (Not for sports or TV like my father, but for high-tech computer patents.) It's fine with Cameron, he can't hear me anyway, or if he does, none of this makes much of an impression. He's in a revved-up party mood, leaning close to me and smiling.

"Let me get you a beer, Fran—did you say 'Francesca'? That's a pretty name." I don't tell Cameron that I hate beer, even the smell, the sharp taste like stinging that makes me want to sneeze; for sure I don't tell Cameron that my parents would be madder than hell if they knew I was even at a party where "drinking" was going on. It's like, though I definitely pro-

to nudge into sb. to run/bump into sb. **pumpkin** *Kürbis* **to subside** to diminish, recede **juvenile** young **to mumble** to speak indistinctly **Vashon Island** the largest island of Puget Sound **executive** (n) chief, director **to jostle** to bump against **revved-up** full of go, *aufgedreht*

mised them that I wouldn't drink "anything alcoholic" or "experiment" with drugs in any way, shape, or form, suddenly here I am at a party, with people I don't know, older than me by years, and everything I'd promised and resolved just melted away.

Cameron grabs my hand, leads me somewhere. The music is so loud now, it's like the eye of a tornado. Wild! I've never been at a party so *cool.* Cameron is talking to me and I'm grinning and saying yes not knowing what we're talking about except it's making me laugh. I'm at this party with a guy of maybe eighteen whom I don't know but we're getting along really well, and people are dancing and it's this bumpy shrieking-giggly freaky stuff that's easy to do, you just wriggle like a snake. And it's like Franky Pierson has been transformed. Like I am a totally different girl because of Cameron. As if he'd snapped his fingers and made me good-looking and sexy where before I was gawky and self-conscious. And I can dance, I'm loose-jointed and limber like a gymnast. Shaking my hips, my arms, thrashing my ponytail from side to side. And Cameron is staring, he's impressed. He likes it that other, older guys are watching me, and are impressed, too.

I catch a glimpse of the girls who brought me to the party, gaping at me like they can't believe their eyes. Little Franky Pierson is *pop-u-lar.*

Maybe by now I'm drunk, but who cares. I'm just floating and grooving and I want the music and dancing never to end.

"Fran-cesca. Thas a pretty name."

Cameron has led me somewhere. I can't stop giggling. My head is a balloon getting bigger and bigger and in danger of bursting, but it's funny, like beer bubbles rising into my nose making me sneeze-sneeze-sneeze.

The music isn't so loud now. I can still hear it, and feel the vibrations, but at a distance.

Cameron is muttering words I can't decipher. We're in a room with a floor-to-ceiling window overlooking the water but it's dark now. I can smell the water, and I can hear the water lapping, but I can't see the water. It's like I'm on a diving board with my eyes shut suddenly afraid of diving. And afraid of falling. Cameron's fingers are strong and hurtful, gripping my rib cage and sort of lifting me. He leans down and begins to

to resolve to decide **bumpy** (adj.) *ruckartig* **shrieking** screaming **giggly** (adj.) *albern, ständig kichernd* **to wriggle** to twist and turn, zigzag **gawky** awkward **loose-jointed** flexible, supple **limber** (adj.) agile **gymnast** *Turner* **to thrash** to hit, whip **to gape** to stare (open-mouthed) **to groove** (sl.) to have fun, enjoy **to decipher** to make sense of **to lap** to splash, surge **rib cage** chest

kiss me. But it isn't like a first, new kiss, it's like a kiss that has already begun, pushy, hard, and his tongue is pressing against my tight-shut lips, everything happening fast. I think *I want this don't I, don't I want this: to be kissed?* Because I can't remember where I am, or who Cameron is. But I know I have to kiss him back. That's what you have to do—kiss back. I'm giggling and shivering and a strange sensation comes over me like parts of my body are going numb. Fingers and toes turning to ice. Panic? But I'm kissing Cameron back; I don't want him to know how scared I am, and how young. His mouth is fleshy and warm, and his hands are moving all over me, hard and practiced. I have a quick weird vision of my brother Todd working out with his weights, bench-pressing, on the treadmill panting and puffing and an oily film of sweat over his face, and if you speak to Todd at such a time he won't hear you, he's so concentrated on his body. This is the way Cameron is. My body can't decide if it's being tickled, or caressed, or—something else, not so nice.

"C-Cameron? Maybe we c-could—"

"Baby, relax. You're so sexy, you're fantastic."

This isn't the first time I've been kissed, exactly. But it's the first time with an older guy, an experienced guy. Someone I don't know who's calling me "Baby" as if he's forgotten my name. He's lifting my tube top, he's touching my breasts, which are the most ticklish part of me, I'm giggling and can't catch my breath, and Cameron's face is giving off heat like he's been running hard, and I'm thinking *Do I want this, is this what I want?* I'm trying to remember what I've been told about safe sex and I'm thinking *Safe sex*? But is this—*sex*?

"Cameron, I guess I don't want to—"

"Baby, come on. You know you do."

I'm panicked but also excited. I guess that's what I feel: excitement? I don't think I'm drunk now. But my stomach is swirling and sickish. My hair is in my face—my ponytail must have come loose. Cameron is pulling my hair. He's kissing me again; it's like his mouth is gnawing at me. I try to push him away, but he doesn't budge. Everything is happening too fast; it's like sinking beneath the surface of the water, taking a breath, swallowing water, suddenly you're panicked and flailing and fighting for your life.

pushy forceful **numb** without feeling **bench-pressing** an exercise or form of weight-lifting in which the lifter lies on his back on a bench lowering and lifting the bar above his chest **treadmill** tiring routine work **to pant** to breathe heavily **to puff** to fight for breath **to caress** to pet, embrace **to gnaw** to chew, bite **to budge** to move, give way **to flail** to struggle

Cameron is pushing me down onto something. Not a bed or a sofa, it feels like a table. Something hard, the edge cutting into my thigh. He's still calling me "Baby," but his tone isn't so friendly now. Like he's coaxing an animal to come to him he intends to hurt. And he's acting like he's been cheated, too. Like I've been playing some joke on him. He's pinning me down, he's unzipped his pants, he's fumbling and panting and pulling at my shorts like he doesn't care if he rips them, and I want to scream but his forearm is pressing against my throat. "Goddamn you, quit playing games. You little—"

I'm struggling hard. I try to scream. I don't know what to do.

Then, suddenly: I know. It's like a match being struck. My knee comes up, hard. I catch this guy in the pit of his belly, right in his groin. He gives a strangled cry and goes limp—it happens in an instant. I'm saying, "Leave me alone! Get off me!" Still I'm on my back, but kicking like crazy. It's like I'm propelling myself across the pool using just my legs, and my legs are strong from years of swimming and running. Maybe I look skinny but I'm strong, the way a cat is strong. Cameron's weight is on me but I'm able to slide out from beneath him, hitting him however I can, and slashing at him with even my teeth. My teeth!

This scares Cameron, I guess. He's groaning and cursing me, holding himself tenderly between the legs. He's staring at me saying, "You f-freak! You should see your eyes! Freaky green eyes! You're *crazy*!"

A wild laugh comes out of my mouth. It's like this guy has seen into my soul.

I'm free of him by now, and running. Out of the room, along a corridor, past potted ferns and Indian masks hanging on a wall, I'm like a wild animal seeking a way out of a maze, here's a door, suddenly I'm outside in the fresh air, and I'm safe.

It's dark and misty and I smell Puget Sound and I'm drawing in great gulps of air like I've been drowning.

But now I'm SAFE.

I'm a good runner. I love to run almost as much as I love to swim. So I jog home along the shore road, trying to stay out of the way of traffic, my hair streaming and blowing down my back. Probably I look like a maniac to people driving past. But I'm feeling *so good*. It isn't like you'd ex-

thigh (n) the upper part of the human leg **to coax** to persuade, sweet-talk **pit of one's belly** the lower part of the torso **groin** (n) *Leistengegend* **to go limp** to lose one's strength **skinny** thin **to slash at sb.** here: to attack sb. fiercely **to groan** to grumble **maze** (n) *Irrgarten* **to draw in gulps of air** here: to struggle for air **maniac** madwoman/madman

pect, I don't even think, *I was almost raped, oh God*, instead I'm thinking how happy I am, and how lucky. My mother said how she'd been more lucky than smart at my age, but I'm thinking I was lucky and smart, too. I fought my assailant, and he couldn't overcome me. I kneed him in the groin, kicked and bit him. I escaped. I hadn't had time even to be afraid. He was a bully and a coward and he'd be worried now, I bet, that I'd tell my parents what had happened, and he'd get into serious trouble.

Well, I wouldn't tell. It's enough to have escaped.

FREAKY GREEN EYES he'd called me.

FREAKY GREEN EYES saved my life.

TWO
the celebration: april 18

The good news was: Dad's new contract with the network had come through.

The less-than-good news was: Mom wasn't here to celebrate with us, like other times.

Dad was saying, "I've worked hard for this, and I think I deserve it. I'm just so grateful. I've been blessed. And you kids . . ." We loved Dad when he was like this, when he'd hug us so hard, our ribs practically cracked. "Well! What I'm trying to say is—the one thing that matters is family. A man's family is his honor. It means far more to him than worldly reputation. The way the world knows him. His dignity, his respect. We love one another, we Piersons, and we stick together, right? We're a *team*."

Dad spoke in this warm, tremulous voice as he did on TV when an athlete or a team had done something spectacular. As a former football star, Reid Pierson identified with athletes the way most sportscasters never could. His boyish, battered good looks and one-hundred-watt smile had made him a favorite of TV sports fans, and when we saw him on TV, it was just so unbelievable, *he was our dad*.

There was this fantastic tenth birthday of mine, when Dad was on TV covering a game in Florida for the network, and Mom had made a big bowl of hot buttered popcorn, and my big brother, Todd, and my little

assailant attacker **bully** (n) sb. who uses his strength to hurt or frighten weaker people **network** radio, TV **tremulous** shaky, trembling **battered** damaged, *(leicht) ramponiert* **to cover** to report

sister, Samantha, and I were sitting with her in the family room watching the program, and there was Reid Pierson looking so handsome and happy, and just before a station break, he winked at the camera and said, "Happy birthday, Franky!"—real quick, it went so fast probably nobody heard it except us. *Happy birthday, Franky.*

Sure, I was proud. I'm only human. I'd have liked Dad to be home for my birthday but it was pretty decent compensation, that Reid Pierson was my father, and could wink at me via TV and wish me a happy birthday.

Dad was one to celebrate things. What he called his Good News Bonanzas. Always there would be a Good News Celebration. A huge Chinese banquet, for instance. Dad loved getting on the phone and ordering enough food for a dozen people, and if Mom was in the room, she'd laugh (just a little anxiously, sometimes) and protest, "Oh, honey, who's going to eat *all that*?"

Today, Mom wasn't with us. I knew that Dad was pissed, I'd overheard them "discussing" the subject that morning. It must have been that Dad knew his good news was imminent, though he'd been secretive about telling us (for in the world of public relations and press releases you were bound to secrecy until certain facts were publicly acknowledged), so he didn't like it at all that Mom was going to an arts-and-crafts fair in Santa Barbara, California. Not just that Mom would be absent from our Good News Celebration, but Dad disapproved of his wife being involved with "artsy-craftsy" people he described as "menopausal females" and "gay boys"—categories of human beings to be scorned.

I knew that Dad had put pressure on Mom to cancel her trip, like he'd pressured her into canceling a previous trip to Vancouver, B.C., back in January. That time, there hadn't been any special Good News occasion, just that Dad wanted Mom home for the weekend. He traveled so much for his TV job, he said he depended on Mom being home when he was home. "Darling, it's my job that finances our elegant lifestyle. And you enjoy our lifestyle, don't you?"

Mom had said quickly, "Reid, you know I do. Of course I—"

"The least I can expect from my wife is emotional support, I guess?"

decent ['di:sənt] proper, appropriate **compensation** *Entschädigung* **banquet** feast, dinner **pissed** AE (vulg.) furious **imminent** (adj.) about to happen, close **secretive** keeping things secret **release** (n) announcement **secrecy** the practice of keeping a secret **to disapprove of** to find unacceptable **artsy-craftsy** (adj.) (inf.) engaged in handicrafts or decorative arts **menopausal** (adj.) *in den Wechseljahren* **to be scorned** to be worth being looked down upon

"Yes, Reid. You're right."

"Am I right 'with a kiss'?"—this was one of Dad's favorite things he'd say to all of us. You had to laugh at Dad—it wasn't enough for you to agree with him (even when he wasn't one-hundred-percent right) but you had to kiss him on the cheek, too.

Mom had laughed, giving in. Mostly Dad was so funny, you did give in.

You would think that Dad would take us all traveling with him, but actually that wasn't the case. Except for summer vacations of maybe two–three weeks. Because Dad was so busy, and TV competition was "cut-throat" (Dad ran his forefinger across his throat when he uttered these words, with a certain zest like he enjoyed the feel of an invisible razor), he hadn't much time to himself. That was why he disapproved of Mom taking Samantha and me to visit our grandparents in Portland just for a few days. (Something must have happened between Dad and the Connors, because my mom's family almost never came to Seattle to visit us. Nobody ever stayed at our house as guests except sometimes friends or professional acquaintances of Dad's.) I guess Dad was old-fashioned at heart—he didn't like anybody in the family traveling far. Like when Mom's older sister, Vicky, was hospitalized with dysentery in Mexico City a few years ago, Dad said, "See what happens when you leave the U.S.? Especially a lone spinster." Dad was joking but always he was serious, too.

I asked my brother Todd why's it such a big deal with Dad, if Mom goes away for a few days? "It isn't like Mom is flying to the moon," I said. "She's coming right back."

But Todd always took Dad's side in any disagreement. He said, with this put-upon-older-brother expression of his, "'Cause Dad wants Mom home." Like that was all it was: so simple.

Anyway, Mom had left for Santa Barbara that morning. At the time of the Good News Celebration she was one thousand miles south of Seattle. When she called home, she said, sounding guilty as a naughty little girl, "It's summer here, can you believe it? The ocean is shimmering and beautiful. I've been walking barefoot along the beach. . . ."

Here it was cold, misty, and mushroom gray, like there was a sticky membrane over everything. Typical spring weather in the Pacific Northwest.

zest (n) enthusiasm **Portland** largest city in the state of Oregon **to hospitalize** to send sb. to hospital **dysentery** ['disntri] infection of the bowels, *Ruhr* **lone** (adj.) solitary **spinster** (n) here: (derog.) an elderly unmarried woman

I loved Dad's Good News Celebrations. But I couldn't help wishing that Mom had taken me with her.

Just this once! To the Santa Barbara Arts & Crafts Fair. Where we could slip away and walk barefoot along the beach . . .

On the phone, Mom had said hesitantly, "Francesca, please say hello and love to your father, will you? I can't seem to reach him through his office or cell phone. He hates e-mail messages unless they're business. But he knows how proud I am of him. . . . Francesca?"

"Sure, Mom. I'll tell him."

There was something strange about this conversation. I didn't want to think about it at the time. An almost inaudible quavering sound to Mom's voice. *Like she is pleading with me. Why?*

"Love ya, honey!"

"Love you, Mom."

It was our usual sign-off. It was really hard for Mom and me to say "love" like we meant it, even when we meant it; the words had to be jokey, casual.

When I tried to relay Mom's message to Dad that evening, he waved me quiet. "No hypocrisy, 'Fran-ces-ca.' Now that your mother is absent from this house, let's have some integrity, please."

Dad usually called me Franky. When he called me Fran-ces-ca in that emphatic way, it meant that he was mocking Mom, who called me Francesca and never Franky.

Todd heard this and sniggered. He knew what Dad was doing.

Samantha heard and just looked from one of us to the other. Too young to gauge the undercurrents of family politics, my little sister was clueless.

(What was I thinking? I tried not to. If I laughed at Dad's mockery, I'd be betraying Mom. If I frowned, I'd be indicating to Dad that I didn't approve of his sense of humor. So I kept my face stony neutral.)

So I was quiet. And Samantha was quiet. Dad was in one of his flaming moods that could veer in one direction or in another. Like those scary flash fires you see on TV when the Santa Ana blows and causes devastation, houses and thousands of acres of forests burn.

to quaver to tremble **to plead** to beg, implore **casual** offhand, spontaneous **hypocrisy** here: insincerity **integrity** honesty, sincerity **to mock** to ridicule, make fun of **to snigger** to give a suppressed laugh **to gauge** [geidʒ] to determine, judge **undercurrent** undertone **to be clueless** to have no idea **to frown** here: to show anger **to veer** to swing, change suddenly **scary** frightening **Santa Ana** warm dry wind in Southern California in autumn and early winter **devastation** destruction

Todd, who was home from college for the weekend, made up for us. "Hey, Dad, congratulations! One of the guys on the team showed me the piece in *USA Today*. That's cool." Todd had torn out the clipping, which Samantha and I read eagerly. Dad showed us a boxed notice in the morning's *Seattle Times*:

Popular CBS sportscaster Reid Pierson has just signed a five-year contract with the network for a salary his agent describes as "generous, but no more than Reid Pierson is worth." Pierson will be a mainstay of the network team covering next year's summer Olympics.

Dad said happily, "Sky's the limit, kids! You can all come with me."

When I was younger, I used to believe that Dad would actually take me with him on some of his trips. Samantha may still have believed—she was only ten. But Todd and I understood, this was just Dad's way of being generous with us. His words weren't meant to be taken literally.

Except maybe: this time would be different?

"Let the banquet begin. Franky?"

As usual, Dad had ordered enough food for a platoon. He'd grown up, he often said, in "circumstances of hunger"—which meant, I guess, that his family life back in Moose Lake, Washington, hadn't been very happy—and he intended to make up for it. With Mom gone, I was in charge of the kitchen. Heating up food in the microwave, mostly. Samantha helped me carry in the steaming platters, pretending we were waitresses. If Mom had been here, she'd have brought the food out in courses, but Dad wanted everything on the table at once so we could see it: Peking duck, shrimp fried rice, sesame noodles, General T chicken, beef with garlic sauce, pork Szechwan style, lemon chicken, and shrimp Happy Family, plus brown rice and a big platter of Chinese vegetables. Samantha and I had Chinese tea (which we hated—it tasted like old socks) while Dad and Todd were drinking Chinese beer. It was a festive time, but a kind of anxious time, too.

to make up for sb. here: to save sb. from an embarrassing situation *USA Today* a national American newspaper founded in 1982 **clipping** (n) newspaper cutting, extract **boxed** (adj.) in a frame **mainstay** (n) the chief support, central person **platoon** (n) group of soldiers commanded by a lieutenant **in courses** one dish after the other **General T chicken** *Sojahuhn mit Peperoni* **garlic** (n) *Knoblauch*

Just four of us having dinner together in the family room, with Mom gone, felt wrong. And Dad kept making remarks that alluded to this in a sarcastic voice. "Shrimp 'Happy Family.' Well, we think so."

Rabbit, our Jack Russell terrier, was shut away in another part of the house, and once in a while you could hear him whining. Poor Rabbit! When Mom was gone, Rabbit couldn't settle down; he was Mom's dog mostly, though Samantha and I loved him a lot. For some reason, Dad had never liked Rabbit. He complained that Rabbit got on his nerves, so we had to keep Rabbit separate from us as long as Dad was home. (I kept waiting for Dad to ask what that noise was, Rabbit whining and scratching, and say something sarcastic about Mom not taking her precious pet with her, but he didn't.)

As usual when we ate in the family room, Dad switched on the TV so that he and Todd could watch sports. There was a boxing match on a sports channel, on our giant screen that took up half a wall. Lucky for Rabbit, the noise drowned out his noises.

"Wow! Look."

Two tightly muscled young lightweights were pummeling away at each other. One was a lightskinned black with a ferocious scowl, the other was a Hispanic with a badly swollen eye. It was weird to see two young men fierce to hurt each other, about ten feet from where we were sitting eating our Chinese banquet. Dad turned up the volume, and the crowd's roar filled our family room.

If Mom had been home, she wouldn't have liked this. Another sport maybe, basketball or baseball, but not boxing. It was unusual for Dad to watch TV boxing, since he didn't cover boxing matches and it wasn't one of Reid Pierson's sports. Also he disliked listening to sports commentators on rival programs, especially those who'd never been athletes themselves. He called them "phonies"—"hypocrites"— who hadn't earned their jobs as he had.

Dad said, excited, "This is turning into a real fight. These boxers may be lightweights, but they have heavyweight hearts. Know what 'heart' is, girls?"

No need to ask Todd. At six foot one, weighing over two hundred pounds, and an athlete himself, Todd obviously knew.

Of course, Samantha just looked mystified. She'd been playing with her food and now shook her head, "No, Dad . . ."

to allude to to refer to **to whine** to make a high-pitched complaining cry **to pummel** to punch, batter **ferocious** fierce, wild **scowl** (n) an angry look **phon(e)y** (n) (derog.) pretender, charlatan **to mystify** to bewilder, perplex

I sounded like Freaky, giving a stand-up answer: " 'Heart' means super courage. 'Heart' is what an athlete has when he doesn't give up no matter how he's hurt."

Our training coach at Forrester was always urging us, *Be aggressive!*

Freaky Green Eyes was aggressive by nature. But hesitant sometimes to show it.

Dad liked my answer, though. As a star player for the Seahawks, Reid Pierson had displayed "heart" on more than one occasion. Once he was carried writhing in pain from the football field with a torn tendon in his calf.

"Right, Franky. Except it's 'she,' too. A female athlete can have 'heart,' too. Just as a female athlete can choke under pressure and let her team down. It isn't just men who can be heroes or cowards, sweetie. It's women, too."

Dad spoke in that intense way of his that signaled a deeper meaning. *Letting your team down, letting your family down. It comes to the same thing.*

The Freaky thought struck me, to defend Mom. ("Hey! Mom isn't a coward.") But the words choked in my throat. It was Dad's Good News Celebration. It was Dad's time. And maybe, just maybe, I was a little afraid of my father.

Anyway, I knew about "heart." Giving all you have and then some. I participated in school sports myself—soccer, track, swimming, and diving. I guess I was a good swimmer/unpredictable diver, sometimes excellent and sometimes not-so-excellent. Our diving coach at Forrester told me that by the time I was a senior, I'd be one of the best. If I kept practicing.

I used to love sports when I was younger. I guess everything is easier then. As soon as you hit high school, getting on the team is all-important. I practiced swimming and diving sometimes to the point of exhaustion, because I wanted Dad to be proud of me someday. Mom was always telling me not to overdo it—but what did *she* know?

Dad was saying, "Sam-Sam? You understand, don't you? The importance of 'heart.'"

Samantha nodded quickly. "Yes, Daddy." Probably she hadn't any idea what we were talking about. She was a dreamy ten-year-old with a sweet,

stand-up (adj.) direct and sharp **hesitant** uncertain, irresolute **to writhe** to twist **tendon** (n) strong cord joining muscle to bone, *Sehne* **calf** (n) back part of a leg below the knee, *Wade* **to choke** here: to fail at doing sth. **to let sb. down** to fail to support, disappoint sb. **track (-and-fields)** (n) athletic sports

shy disposition and beautiful dark eyes no one would ever call *freaky*. Through dinner she'd been quieter than usual. I guessed she was missing Mom, and she was aware of poor Rabbit whining and lonely in another part of the house.

Dad was urging us to have more of the "delicious food." Samantha protested faintly, but Dad ignored her, spearing pieces and dropping them onto her plate. And there was so much shrimp fried rice, and sesame noodles that were stone cold and sort of squirmy-greasy, I hoped Dad wouldn't make me eat more—I was on the verge of gagging. As usual, Todd had a hearty appetite. He worked out hours every day, so he needed carbohydrates and protein to build up muscle. But I was a finicky eater, and Samantha never ate much at one sitting. I had thought I was fairly hungry when I sat down at the table, but the sugary, gluey Chinese specialties filled me up fast. "This is our celebratory banquet, girls. Your mother couldn't make it but we made it, didn't we! We are not going to waste any of this delicious food." I was tempted to ask why we couldn't save some of it for tomorrow, and the next day, and the next, but I knew better; Dad did not appreciate "smart-aleck" commentary. So I said, "My favorites are the black mushrooms." And I took another serving of mushrooms, on a small mound of brown rice. Samantha, who wasn't so quick or canny, stared in dismay at the platter Dad was pushing at her. When she hesitated, biting her lip, Dad spooned more of the sweet Szechwan pork onto her plate, and the sweeter lemon chicken, which tasted like candy meat. Samantha looked as if she was about to cry.

Todd usually ignored both his sisters, but he seemed to take pity on Samantha now and deflected Dad's interest to the boxing match. "Dad, look! Wow." The black boxer was firing blows at his opponent, forcing the Hispanic boxer backward across the ring. Suddenly then the Hispanic boxer was down, flat on his back on the brightly lighted canvas. The referee stood over him counting in an eerie silence: Dad had turned the volume down. Dad said, "Looks like a knockout. Well done."

While Dad was watching the screen, I began clearing away some of our plates. Deftly I eased Samantha's plate away and carried it with others into the kitchen, and Dad never noticed.

disposition temperament, nature **squirmy-greasy** disgustingly fat **on the verge of** very near to **to gag** almost vomit, *würgen* **finicky** overcritical, hard to please **gluey** sticky **smart-aleck** (n) (inf./derog.) a would-be clever person, *Klugscheisser* **canny** clever, sharp-witted **dismay** (n) alarm **to deflect** to turn aside **eerie** (adj.) mysterious, strange **deftly** (adv.) skilfully

I ran water in the sink to rinse the dishes before putting them into the dishwasher. I took advantage of being out of the family room by running to check on Rabbit, who was frantic with loneliness in my bedroom. "Poor Rabbit! I'm so, so sorry. But you'll be let out soon, I promise." (I'd overheard Dad making plans on his cell phone before dinner, and knew that he was going out for a "nightcap" later in the evening.) Rabbit licked my hands, wriggling his tail like crazy. I thought how sad it was to be a dog, a dumb animal, and not understand that the person you love most in the world, which in this case was my mother, was actually going to come back to you.

Dad's celebratory banquet had to be complete, with fortune cookies and ice cream. Heaping bowls of fudge ripple and butter crunch. When I returned to the family room with our bowls on a tray, the telephone began to ring. It had to be Mom.

We waited for Dad to answer. Todd scratched nervously at his neck. But Dad ignored the ringing phone, watching slow-motion replays of the knockout on TV. Finally after three or four rings I made a move to pick up the receiver, but Dad shook his finger at me without turning. "Francesca. Where are your manners? No phone calls during meals."

"But, Dad, it might be—"

"—might be Mom."

Samantha and I spoke at once.

Dad set his jaws in a way he had that meant the subject was closed. He said nothing, continuing to watch TV as the phone rang another time, then clicked off into voice mail, which we couldn't hear.

I was feeling anxious, jumpy. I just knew it was Mom. And I wondered what she'd be thinking. I wondered what message she would leave. ("Sorry to miss you. Maybe you're all out at the House of Ming? Well, I'll try again later. Love you!")

I expected the boxing program to end, but the replays continued, from different angles including overhead. The Hispanic boxer's right eye was swollen shut, and his face was shining with blood. It was terrible; the close-ups spared nothing. Not only was this twenty-two-year-old boxer hurt, he was being humiliated.

sink (n) *Spülbecken* **to rinse** to wash, clean **frantic** panic-stricken **nightcap** a (usually alcoholic) drink taken before going to bed **fudge ripple** kind of ice cream **butter crunch** toffee **voice mail** highly developed answering machine **jumpy** nervous, ill at ease **House of Ming** name of a Chinese restaurant **close-up** (n) *Nah~, Großaufnahme* **to humiliate** to put to shame, disgrace

Samantha was staring toward the telephone, looking faintly sick.

Todd said suddenly, "Dad, maybe I could try boxing? With a team, there's all these other guys getting in the way."

Dad said, "You? Boxing? You're too slow, son. You're built for football, like your old man."

"I thought you said I was a heavyweight. . . ."

"But you don't have the skills, Todd. Or the reflexes or the drive. Those boxers are hungry to win—they're killers. Your life has been too soft. You're a suburban white kid." It was like Dad to suddenly turn on one of us, as if all along he'd been playing some sort of game, pretending to think we were great. The way he said "suburban white kid" made me shiver.

"Anyway," Dad continued, "you're too old to be trained as a boxer, son."

"Dad, I'm just *twenty*!"

"That's what I said, too old. Boxers start training at fourteen or fifteen. Or younger."

"I could learn," Todd said stubbornly. "I bet I could."

It wasn't a smart move to argue with Dad on any subject, especially sports. Why Todd persisted I don't know. Dad said, "You don't have the killer instinct, Todd. Even mediocre boxers have to have it. Football's different—it's guys on a team. Like brothers." Dad's voice took on a faint, unnerving jeer. "Basically, football is a game."

I would wonder at this remark afterward. Didn't Dad love football, hadn't football been his life? Yet now he seemed to be disparaging it for being only a game.

Todd swallowed a large mouthful of beer. His face was flushed and sulky. Dad took notice of this, laughed, and squeezed Todd's left biceps with approval. "You're in great condition, son, I'm proud of you. Next fall, things are going to happen in your life, I predict."

Todd mumbled. "Sure, Dad."

"Boxing isn't for boys from Yarrow Heights. I wouldn't allow you to step into the ring. Know why?"

Todd shrugged. "Why?"

"Because I'm your dad, and I love you."

I'm your dad, and I love you.

move (n) here: idea **to persist** not give up, continue **mediocre** average, not very good **unnerving** demoralizing, frightening **jeer** (n) mockery, insult **to disparage** to belittle, underestimate **sulky** ill-humoured **to shrug** expressing one's doubt or ignorance by raising and then lowering one's shoulders

Dad turned to Samantha and me, who were looking wistfully on.

"Franky-girl, Sam-Sam: your daddy loves you, too. When you're good girls, not naughty."

We laughed as if we'd been tickled. Almost, I could feel Daddy's strong fingers running up and down my ribs making me squeal with laughter.

For Daddy had not disciplined either of us in some time. You could almost forget there'd been such a time.

Fortune cookies! One by one we broke them open, and read aloud our fortunes with Dad as an audience.

Todd went first. In a high nasal voice meant to mock a Chinese accent, he read: "'Someone who admires you is waiting to be discovered.'" He shrugged, pretending indifference. "That's cool."

Dad said, miming Chinese sagacity, "Time will tell!"

Samantha broke open her cookie and squinted at the tiny red print. "'You bring joy and contentment to all.'" She ducked her head shyly.

Dad said, "That's our Sam-Sam. Somebody's got your number."

My fortune was: "'A calm mind restores calm.'" In a louder voice I re-read: "'A calm mind bestows calm.' Not much of a fortune!"

Dad said severely, "But wise. Somebody's got your number, Fran-cesca."

What did this mean? Did Dad think of me as a troublemaker?

For a paranoid moment I wondered if Dad had planted that fortune in my cookie, to rebuke me. Maybe he sensed Freaky Green Eyes roiling in my heart. *He knows he can't control Freaky.*

The way Dad was looking at me, as if I wasn't his daughter but some impudent red-haired stranger he was sizing up . . .

But Freaky isn't real, I wanted to tell my father. Freaky is just an idea.

Dad broke open his fortune cookie last, and read his fortune in a booming TV voice. "'You will cross a wide water.'" He paused, pondering what this might mean. Then he smiled. "Of course! The Pacific Ocean. And the Atlantic. Round-the-world coverage with Reid Pierson and associates. Perfect."

wistful regretful, sad **fortune cookies** Californian/Chinese biscuit served as a dessert. It contains a paper with prophesies, messages or a Chinese phrase with translation **sagacity** wisdom, (deep) insight **to squint at sth.** *auf etw. schielen* **tiny** very small **to bestow** to grant, give **paranoid** fearful, irrationally anxious **to rebuke sb.** to express severe disapproval to sb. **to roil** here: to agitate, stir **impudent** impertinent **size up** (inf.) form an opinion of sb/sth **booming** (adj.) sonorous **to ponder** to think about

I saw a lone cookie remaining on the plate. Mom's.

Our usual order from the House of Ming was for five people, so they'd sent over five fortune cookies.

Samantha naively pointed at the cookie, just discovering it.

"That's Mom's. We can save it for her."

Dad snatched the cookie up. He was making an effort to smile.

"No, Sam-Sam. In your mother's absence, an emissary will read it for her."

Dad tore off the cellophane wrapper, broke the cookie in two, drew out the little fortune, and read, in his TV voice: "'You will—cross a wide water.'" There was a pause. Todd and I exchanged a nervous glance, the first rapport we'd had in a long time. A strange expression came over our father's face as if he'd been insulted, or maybe it was only a joke—an audience was watching him keenly to see how he would react. He laughed. "Well! A coincidence. Must be the fortune-teller has run out of original ideas, we're into reruns. Your mother and I have the identical fortune, it seems. But we won't have the identical future." Dad broke the cookie into several pieces and ate it, slowly.

We all ate our cookies, which were slightly stale and hadn't much taste.

THREE
the quarrel: may 5

Something is going to happen.

The worst you can think, regarding your parents: something has already happened. What?

That night. I lie awake listening.

No. I am not listening. It's thunder, pelting rain. Mixed with my dreams.

In another part of the house. Muffled, through the walls. A raised voice. Dad's voice. Controlled, reasonable. *Why can't you, why won't you, I'm warning you.* The words are indistinct, but the rhythm of the voice is unmistakable.

emissary delegate, representative **rapport** (n) close relationship **rerun** (n) repeat **stale** (adj.) dry **pelting rain** pouring with rain **to muffle** to suppress, make indistinct

The second voice, the weaker voice. Highpitched, a woman's voice. I feel scorn for it. The deeper voice rolls over it, obliterates it. Like thunder rolling across the sky.

I'm awake, sitting up in bed. Kicking at the covers. It was nothing, only thunder. Now rain is pelting against my windows. Where I left a window partly open, rain is being blown inside, wetting papers strewn across my desk.

It was nothing. Only thunder.

In the bathroom mirror Freaky Green Eyes glares at me. I feel a crazy urge to claw at those eyes.

In the morning Samantha came shyly into my room. I looked up, surprised to see her. My room is off-limits, this time of morning. I'm half dressed, brushing at my flyaway hair. "Franky? I heard them again last night. I couldn't sleep."

Samantha looked at me anxiously. I could see her eyelids trembling. I wanted to hug her, quick. Hide my face against her hair, so she couldn't see it.

At the same time, I couldn't show her that I was scared. She'd asked me about Dad and Mom in the past, since that weekend Mom went to Santa Barbara, and always I said it was nothing much, probably nothing much, you know how Daddy is, Daddy has a temper but it dies down fast, Daddy will kiss and make up, Daddy loves us. The way Samantha was watching my face, I knew I had to be very careful. I took the occasion to brush her hair, which needed it. I said, "I don't think so, Samantha. I didn't hear anything. It must have been a dream." I paused, thinking. "Maybe it was thunder. There was a storm last night."

Morning mist pressed against the windows. You could see a few evergreens, and Lake Washington vague and shimmering, but nothing more. Samantha winced when my hairbrush hit a snarl. "Franky, I know what dreams are! This wasn't a dream, and it wasn't thunder. I heard Daddy shouting at Mom. He said—"

I pushed Samantha from me. Her hot, squirmy little body. I wanted to press my hands over my ears. I didn't want this, not before

to obliterate to blot out, deaden **covers** (n) bedclothes **to claw** to scratch **off-limits** AE not allowed to be entered by sb. **Santa Barbara** town in California 85 miles northwest of Los Angeles, on the Pacific coast **to make up** to be friends again **to wince** to grimace **snarl** (n) knot **squirmy** (adj.) here: huddled up, cowered

school. Not on a busy morning when already I had too much to think about.

I heard myself say, "Ask Mom, then. Ask Mom about it. She's causing this. Ask Mom!"

But Samantha couldn't. And I couldn't. And Mom wouldn't have told us anyway. Smiling that smile of hers, brave, stubborn, breathless all that spring as if her pulse was fast, like she'd been running.

I guess I did blame Mom. She provoked Dad with her attitude, and Dad, being Reid Pierson, couldn't help but react. On TV he was super cheerful, but around the house, well—he could be moody. That was just Dad's personality.

It seemed to happen gradually. Or maybe I wasn't old enough to notice. But around the time I was in eighth grade, the tension began to show. Mom was losing her enthusiasm for being Mrs. Reid Pierson in public. She'd never felt comfortable at the gigantic banquets and cocktail receptions, fund-raisers that were always honoring Reid Pierson and other celebrities in order to sell tickets; she'd try to make a joke of how miserable she was amid swarms of strangers in tuxedos and long dresses eager to shake the hand of Reid Pierson and get his autograph, but looking through Krista Pierson as if she didn't exist. Still, for about fourteen years she'd gone with Dad to such events, and she'd looked the part of Reid Pierson's beautiful wife, Krista, who'd once been a TV news announcer herself for a Portland station. Now I overheard Mom say to Dad, "This party tonight! I don't want to go, honey. I'm just not in the mood for packs of people. Please can I stay home?" and Dad said, "No, darling. You can't. You're my date, see?" Dad was treating this as a joke, or a game. It was like they were playing Ping-Pong in the family room.

Mom said, "Of course it's wonderful that you're being honored, and I know it's for a good cause, but I'd so much rather stay home with the girls and work a little in my studio. Tomorrow—"

"Krista, do you even remember what tonight's occasion is?"

"The Medical Center? Or—no, United Charities?"

Coldly Dad said, "Check your calendar. Get your facts straight."

"Honey, it doesn't matter what it is. The same people are always there, saying the same kinds of things. The amplification is deafening, everyone drinks too much, it won't break up until past eleven P.M. Please can't I—"

tuxedos AE *Smoking* **amplification** here: noise level **deafening** (adj.) extremely loud

Dad was sounding patient, but exasperated. I was backing away, not wanting to hear how this would end. My heart had begun to beat, hard, in worry for Mom. "It's the *Seattle Times* 'Outstanding Citizens of the Year' awards. They only choose eight people. It will make the front page of the paper—it's a very big deal. And it would look peculiar if Reid Pierson came by himself. If his wife, Krista, didn't give a damn about this award."

Mom protested, "Of course I care, Reid. I do care. I'm proud of you. But no one would miss me. That's why I want to stay home tonight. I'd like to make an early dinner for Francesca and Samantha, just the three of us. It seems we never see enough of one another any longer, and suddenly they'll be gone, like Todd. The house will be empty, I'll be—"

"Lonely? With just your husband?"

"Honey, you're always gone. And when you're home, you're going out every evening. It's no kind of life, and it's getting worse. And I—I'm not the person you married any longer. I'm not twenty-two years old."

"No, you're not. You're pushing forty. You'd better be grateful you have a husband who wants you to appear in public with him, who's still in love with you. Lots of people we know, that isn't any longer the case with their marriages."

Mom said, hurt, "Reid, what do you mean? Are you—threatening me?"

"No, darling. Why should I 'threaten' you? Have I ever threatened you, even with the truth?"

"What—is that supposed to mean?"

"You're a smart woman, Krista. So you think. With your artsy new friends whose 'values' are so superior to mine. You should be able to figure out certain facts for yourself."

There was a pause. Some movement. I heard a muffled sound I didn't want to think was Mom crying.

By this time I was almost out of earshot of their voices. Making my escape. Still I heard Dad's voice raised now, and angry. "Why the hell did you marry Reid Pierson, if you don't want to be Reid Pierson's fucking wife?"

Pressing my hands against my ears. Even Freaky wasn't in a mood to hear.

Crossing over. That was what my mother was doing, too. Last winter, spring, summer. I guess I didn't want to know. I didn't want to think where it might lead, how some of us might be hurt and left behind.

to not give a damn about sb. / sth. (inf.) to not care at all about sb./sth. **to figure out** to work out **out of earshot** where one cannot be heard

FOUR
the quarrel: may 29

The scarfs Mom began wearing. Beautiful brightcolored silky scarfs. And shawls. And long-sleeved shirts, pullovers. Sometimes the sleeves drooped to her wrists, hiding her wrists.

Hiding what? Bruises on her wrists, on her neck and upper arms? Angry red welts made by a man's strong fingers?

I could not ask. The words gathered in my throat but stuck there. In Mom's presence I began to be very quiet. And Mom was becoming ever more quiet with me.

***

Always it was late night, my sleepless time when I sent e-mail messages in my head. And sometimes, maybe a little desperate, I'd get out of bed and check my messages (mostly there were none: I checked my messages compulsively and answered them at once) and send one, as I did to Todd. How many times, I'd be ashamed to recount.

Hi, Todd --

Haven't heard from you in a while & hope things are OK there.

Just wondered if you knew what might be/is happening between Dad & Mom these days. (I guess Dad would tell you if anyone.)

Franky

Another night—

Todd, hi!
Just me checking in. It's kind of lonely here.

Dad's away for four days in Atlanta. (Baseball?)
Wondering if you're in touch with him?

Wondering if you knew what might be/ is happening between Dad & Mom? If anything.

(kid sister) Franky

scarf piece of cloth worn around one's neck, head or shoulder **shawl** piece of cloth worn around the shoulders or head **bruise** (n) injury, black and blue mark **welt** (n) mark left on the skin by a heavy blow or pressure **compulsively** (adv.) as if driven by a desire impossible to control

I know, it was pathetic. Signing my name like that. Lots of things I did, those months, were pretty pathetic.

Todd never replied to any of my e-mail messages. I guess I knew in my heart that he wouldn't.

You'd have to have a big brother to understand.

It used to be, when I was little, that Todd was my friend. Then he got obsessed with high school sports, which took up all his spare time. There were months—years, I guess—when I hardly saw Todd; he was in and out of the house, always in a hurry, only taking time to sit down for a meal if Dad was home. Depending upon how Todd was getting along with Dad, that's how Todd would get along with Mom, Samantha, and me. Then he left home, began college at Washington State in Pullman, joined the biggest jock fraternity (where, he said, "Reid Pierson is a household word"), and rarely came home for weekends. And when he did, he didn't have time for me.

Mom wasn't Todd's actual—biological—mother. Maybe that explains Todd's estrangement. His mother (Dad's first wife) had died a long time ago, and no one ever spoke of her. So Todd might have thought of Mom, Samantha, and me as partial relatives, not whole.

In the family, only Dad was real to Todd.

At first Mom complained, smiling, that she never saw her "big, handsome son" any longer. Todd never confided in her as he used to do, and he wouldn't allow her to come into his room, or tousle his hair and tease him. Saying good-bye, Todd only just let himself be hugged and kissed, standing stiff as a soldier at attention. This past year, Mom had stopped joking. If she spoke of Todd at all, she sounded hurt, and baffled.

Through May, Mom was smiling. The Freaky thought came to me to ask, *Is that smile stapled onto your face, Mom? Does it hurt?* I wanted to ask if she smiled like that while she was sleeping. If someone shone a flashlight into her face, waking her, would she be smiling like that? I wanted to ask, but I didn't.

Pullman city in southeastern Washington with a well-known university (WSU) **jock** AE (inf.) sportsman **fraternity** club at an American university with only male members **estrangement** turning away, alienation **to confide in** to open one's heart to **to tousle** to make sb.'s hair look untidy **to baffle** to perplex, disconcert **to staple onto** to fasten, fix to.

I began to resent Mom, that she was acting so strange. I resented worrying about her, I guess. Your mother is supposed to worry about *you*, not the other way around!

There was a new stiffness between us. On my part, anyway. I wasn't her little Francesca any longer; she couldn't expect me to snuggle up to her and behave like Samantha. I knew she was sensing a change in my attitude, but she didn't say anything for a while. (That was like Mom, too. Not to speak of something that's bothering her, like possibly it will go away.) But one day she broke down and asked if something was wrong. "You seem so . . . withdrawn, honey. You haven't spoken five words to me since you've gotten into this car."

We were driving home to Yarrow Heights, same as usual. Mom had swung by Forrester to pick me up after swim practice. She'd been doing other errands, too; the rear of the station wagon was crammed with art supplies.

My father hated the smell of acrylic paints and modeling clay. On my mother's fingers and beneath her short-filed nails, what looked liked dried mud.

For God's sake, Krista. You look like a field worker.

I was slouched in the passenger seat. Sliding a Laurie Anderson CD into the tape deck, the one that begins with eerie whale music.

"Okay, Mom. 'Five words to me.'"

Mom laughed, sounding a little startled.

We listened to Laurie Anderson's breathy voice. Strange undersea sounds. It suited the atmosphere of Seattle in May: mist, threat-of-rain, rain.

I've seen whales in the ocean. Not many, but a few. Killer whales, so-called. In the Juan de Fuca Strait (between northern Washington and British Columbia) and in the ocean, a forty-minute drive to the west. It's awesome! When you see the whales surface, leap, frolic in the glassy-green water, your heart lifts. You stare and stare at the water waiting for whales to reappear.

Mom murmured something approving about the music. It was Mom's kind of music, too. Then she turned the volume down so we could talk.

"How was swim practice?"

to resent sb. to dislike, feel bitter about sb. **to snuggle up to sb.** *sich kuscheln, anschmiegen* **errand** (n) task, shopping **to slouch** sit in a lazy way **Laurie Anderson** American experimental performance artist and musician **awesome** breathtaking **to frolic** to play and move about in a lively way

"Okay."
"Were you diving?"
"No. Not today."
(I had been diving, actually. I mean, I'd tried. My knees were weak. I had trouble concentrating. "Not a diving day" is what we call it, diplomatically.)
Mom drove. I wasn't looking in her direction. Yet I could see that her smile was beginning to slide on one side, as if the staples there had loosened. Her eyes (bloodshot, but I wasn't going to look) seemed to pucker as she stared into the rearview mirror, driving a little more jerkily than usual. As if this familiar way home to our house on Vinland Circle wasn't so familiar to her; there might be surprises. Mom said hesitantly, "I wonder if you're distracted by something, Francesca. At school, or . . ." But here Mom paused. Not wanting to say *at home*.
I said, annoyed, "Mom, I really don't like 'Francesca.' It's so pretentious. Like, are we Italian or something? Samantha is bad enough—it's such a cliché. But Francesca." I sighed. I turned the CD volume up, to hear Laurie Anderson singing about somebody she loved slipping away.
Mom seemed hurt, so I added, "Everybody calls me Franky, y'know? Like it suits me. Who I am."
I'd have liked to tell Mom about Freaky. But not today.
"Oh, we've been through this a thousand times!" Mom tried to laugh. "All right, 'Franky.' If that's how you wish to be perceived."
How I wished to be perceived? I'd never thought of it that way. Always I'd assumed that other people called you what they chose to call you, beginning with your parents, and you had no choice.
I said, "Even my teachers call me Franky, Mom. Except if they're scolding."
Mom tried to laugh. "Well. 'Franky.' I've been noticing that you've been unusually quiet lately. Since I went to Santa Barbara . . . you've been withdrawn. I hope there isn't some connection?"
I squirmed in my seat. "Mom, no."
"The other day, when I drove Twyla and Jenn home, I noticed you were so quiet, they did all the talking. . . ." Mom hesitated, knowing this was dangerous territory. "I hope you always feel that you can talk to me, Francesca. I mean, Franky. If . . ."

to pucker to wrinkle, *sich zusammenziehen* **jerky** (adj.) bumpy, not smooth **pretentious** affected, pompous **to squirm** to twist one's body from side to side because of feeling uncomfortable

"Sure, Mom. Okay."

Something very weird had happened at Santa Barbara, I think. Dad was gone that Saturday morning saying he had "emergency business" in L.A., but from things I overheard after Mom returned, I guess he'd gone to the arts-and-crafts fair to check on her; he hadn't made contact with her, only just "spied" on her. Then he'd returned.

I guess this was what happened. There was nobody I could ask.

I'd overheard Dad say *Your lezzie friends. Palling around with your lezzie friends. I saw you.* What Mom replied I had not heard.

Mom was telling me blah blah blah. When she'd been my age blah blah. In St. Helens, Oregon. As if I didn't know. Her small-town background she'd loved. I wanted to turn the CD volume up high to drown out her voice.

No. I wanted to squeeze over against her and nudge her. Like I'd done all the time when I was little. Nudging Mom, pushing against her so she'd pull me onto her lap. "My big girl," she'd say, laughing. "My big beautiful girl." This was fine for Samantha, still; she was only ten. But not for Franky, who wanted to smooth away the smile lines at the corners of Mom's mouth and eyes, which looked as if they'd been made by tiny knife blades.

I wanted to grab her hands. Tell her her hands were beautiful. Even with the unglamorous short nails. Even if there were telltale ridges of clay or paint beneath them.

The Freaky impulse came to me, to pull away the turquoise scarf Mom had knotted so carefully around her throat.

At the same time I was wishing I could escape somewhere. At least that I was sixteen and had my driver's license. (Dad had promised me my own car, if I was a "good girl.") That way I wouldn't be so damned dependent on Mom to drive me places. It was too intimate, this mother-daughter thing. Too much!

By the time Mom turned into our driveway, I had my hand on the door handle. By the time she braked to a stop, I was halfway out, dragging my backpack behind me. I called back over my shoulder in a perfectly innocent not-blaming Franky voice, "Mom, I'm fine. I'm great. I have my own life, okay? Like you have yours."

lezzie AE (adj. sl.) lesbian **to pal around with sb.** AE to associate with sb. as a friend **to nudge** to give sb. a gentle push (with your elbow) **unglamorous** unattractive **telltale** (adj.) revealing **ridge** (n) here: trace **turquoise** (adj.) *türkisfarben*

The first time Twyla Lee came home with me to have dinner and stay the night at our house, she looked around, rolled her eyes, and whispered in my ear, "This is cool, Franky. But do you guys actually *live here*?"

Twyla was joking of course. The Lees' own house was pretty special. But I knew what she meant.

When my father began to be really successful in his TV career, he wanted a new house custom built for him and his family. He purchased a lot in Yarrow Heights overlooking Lake Washington and the Evergreen Floating Bridge, a few miles from Seattle to the west. Dazzling lights after dark. When you could see through the mist.

The house was designed by a famous Japanese American Seattle architect. It's what is called "postmodernist," meaning it doesn't look like a house exactly, more like a small high-tech building. Glass walls, skylights, poured concrete, some chilly glaring metal like pewter. There are tubular glass-walled "galleries"—not old-fashioned halls. There are module units, not rooms. There are sliding Japanese screens that "create" rooms, or "remove" rooms. The rooms are echo chambers with "minimalist" furnishings: metallic chairs, translucent tables, halogen lamps that give off a faint blue light. Neutral nothing colors like faded black, pebble gray, sickly white. Low, long sofas with scattered dwarf cushions. What seem like acres of bare gleaming tile, dull black, dead white, with only incidental rugs. Even the lighting fixtures are minimalist, recessed in the walls and ceilings, so they seem to cast shadows in all directions. My mother had hoped to furnish the house herself, but my father insisted upon the most fashionable Seattle interior decorator.

My father said they couldn't afford to make any mistakes. The "eyes of the world" would be on them, quick to mock and deride if they slipped up.

In one of the so-called galleries Dad's football trophies and photographs with fellow athletes and celebrities were displayed. It was pretty spectacular: photos of Reid Pierson shaking hands with Seattle politicians, the governor, even then-president Bill Clinton at the White House. Both Reid

custom built built according to the buyer's specifications **Evergreen (Point) Floating Bridge** bridge that links Seattle with its environments. It is 1.4 miles long **dazzling** extremely bright **poured concrete** *Schüttbeton* **pewter** (n) *Zinn* **sliding screen** here: door that opens by moving to one side **translucent** semi-transparent **pebble** (n) small round stone **sickly** here: pale **dwarf** (adj.) miniature, small **incidental** sporadic, here and there **rug** (n) piece of cloth or wool that covers a part of the floor **recessed** sunk, *eingelassen* **to deride** to make fun of, laugh **to slip up** to make a mistake

Pierson and Bill Clinton were good-looking, confident men smiling with their earnest, boyish appeal into the camera. Dad marveled at Clinton's charisma, which he said you had to experience first-hand to appreciate. Dad said, "You couldn't help but love that man. You can see why, if people love you enough, they'll forgive you anything."

I was in eighth grade when The Pierson Home in Yarrow Heights, Washington, was featured in *Seattle Life*, a new student at the preppy Forrester Academy, with almost no friends; overnight, even older students took notice of me, singling me out to say they'd seen the article in the magazine and were impressed by it. I have to admit I was flattered. ("And your dad is Reid Pierson, what's that *like*?") I'd just started ninth grade when the house was featured in *Architectural Digest*, with dramatically posed shots of Reid Pierson (in a tuxedo) and his wife, Krista Pierson (in a skintight black silk dress, shoulderlength red hair glossy as fire), amid the minimalist furniture, with a glimpse of Lake Washington in the background; this time, even teachers I didn't have sought me out, as well as the school headmaster, to tell me they'd seen the article and were impressed. Mr Whitney, the headmaster, had already met my mother, of course, but not my father. Earnestly he said, "Tell your father I've always been a fan, Francesca. Going back to his Seahawks days. Tell him I hope he'll drop by Forrester someday soon."

That was about eighteen months ago. Dad hasn't gotten to Forrester yet, but every time Mr Whitney sees me, he says, "Francesca! Remember, the invitation is always open."

Actually, the postmodernist look is mostly for show, on the first floor in what the architect called the "public space" of the house. On the lower floor, our "private space" rooms are more or less normal. Bedrooms, guest rooms, bathrooms, closets. (Though not enough closets.) Here things were built to a smaller scale, as if the architect hadn't any interest in where his clients might actually live.

We'd been living in an older, smaller house closer to downtown Seattle, in what was called an ethnically diverse neighborhood. I had lots of friends there and hated to move. (And I hated the new house. I cried and sulked for days.) Mom kept saying, "It's an adventure! It's like a spaceship." We were lucky Dad allowed Mom to furnish the lower-floor rooms herself.

confident optimistic **to marvel** to be amazed **to feature** to present **preppy** AE (adj. inf.) chic, smart **to single sb. out** to select, pick out **glossy** shiny, gleaming **glimpse** (n) short, quick look **to drop by** to pay a casual, short visit to sb. or a place **to sulk** to be in a bad mood

Last year Mom converted a room in the guest wing into a small studio. She was taking classes in pottery, weaving, and painting. Her studio wasn't large and didn't have a spectacular view of the lake, but it had a skylight, and Samantha and I had fun helping Mom paint the walls a warm pale yellow so there was the feeling in Mom's studio that the sun was shining, or almost, on even our gloomiest winter days.

In the Pacific Northwest rain forest, which is where we live, it can rain for weeks at a time. No sun. And if the sun appears, it can disappear within seconds.

Dad had allowed Mom to convert the room into a studio, but he'd never liked the idea. The more time Mom spent at home, in that studio, the less time she had for the kinds of socializing he thought a wife of his should be doing, like lunching with the well-to-do women who ran such organizations as the Friends of the Seattle Opera and United Charities. He complained that, far away at the other end of the house where their bedroom was, he could smell paint fumes. They gave him a sinus headache, damn it! When Mom showed him the first weavings and clay pots she'd made, which Samantha and I thought were very beautiful, Dad just smiled and shook his head like an indulgent father. "This is what you've been doing, Krista? They're fine. Great." That was all he said. Mom was hurt but tried not to show it.

Soon she stopped showing Dad her new work, even when she was able to place it in a local gallery and began selling it. And Dad never asked about it, or visited Mom's cozy studio.

Lots of things I'd always told my mom I'd never have told my dad. But lately I wasn't telling Mom things, either. Since Freaky entered my heart, last July on Puget Sound. I wondered if Freaky would have come to me if it hadn't been for Cameron; if I hadn't almost made a terrible mistake and become desperate. *You should see your eyes! Freaky green eyes! You're crazy!* But I wasn't crazy, I knew that. I was stronger, I was empowered. I liked myself better than I ever had before, since I was a small child. Weird thoughts came to me, like *You belong in this world, just like everyone else. Except you're Freaky Green Eyes, so you know it.*

Since starting my period, I'd been kind of disgusted with myself, or ashamed of myself, I don't know. But since Freaky, I didn't feel that way.

to socialize to have people round, meet people **sinus** (anat.) *Nebenhöhle* **indulgent** tolerant, permissive **cozy** comfortable, homely **to be empowered** to be given more control over one's life, emancipated

I remembered how I'd escaped from Cameron, how I'd jogged back home in the rain, so happy. I stood in front of my bedroom mirror naked, as I'd never done before, liking my hard little breasts with the dimple-nipples, and the pale-flamy swath of silky hairs at my crotch, and my lean muscled swimmer's legs, even my long, narrow, toadstool-white feet. I didn't stare or ogle, I just looked at myself like you'd look at a flower, or a tree, or an animal, anything natural, unclothed. Especially, though, I did admire my carroty-red hair, which I was letting grow long, frizzy and static with electricity, past my shoulders. Most of the time I fastened it into a ponytail to keep it out of my face. (Mom gave me a silver clasp for the ponytail, inlaid with turquoise stones.) Like my eyes, it was Freaky's special sign. But I felt good about it, not secretive.

Was I sad that I no longer told my mother the things that mattered most to me? Twyla said it was the same with her. "Suddenly, one day, I heard myself lying to my mother. Not for any special reason—just I didn't want her to know my heart."

I said to Twyla, "I don't think I'd ever want anybody to know my heart. Who could you trust?"

We thought about that. You were supposed to be able to trust people you fell in love with, but that could be risky: people fall out of love all the time. Twyla said, wryly, "Your girl friend."

It was true. Maybe. If there was anybody I could trust, it would be a close girl friend like Twyla. But that was risky, too.

"Francesca?"

I was in my room, at my computer but daydreaming. Staring out the window at the lead-colored lake and thinking of Twyla, and my other friends I didn't seem to have much to say to lately. Maybe it was what Mom said: I was "withdrawn."

Is "withdrawn" the same as "depressed"? Or just a mood?

Mom pushed my door open a few inches, hesitantly. She pushed her head inside. "Hon? Are you busy? Can you talk?"

A huge sigh ballooned in my chest.

"Sure, Mom. Come in."

I hated being invaded like this. Though I'd known Mom would come looking for me. She wasn't one to let things go.

dimple (adj.) here: concave, *eingezogen* **swath** (n) here: triangle **crotch** (n) lap, *Schritt* **toadstool** *Giftpilz* **to ogle** to stare, gaze at **secretive** (adj.) uncommunicative **wryly** (adv.) ironically, mockingly **lead** [led] (n) Blei

Still wearing the turquoise scarf. And a longsleeved shirt, buttoned to the cuffs. Her eyes were lightly threaded with blood; the rims looked reddened. "Can I sit down? You're not doing homework, are you?"

"Sort of," I lied. "But I can talk, sure."

This was when Mom first spoke of Skagit Harbor. Her "cabin" there: did I remember it?

Skagit Harbor is an old fishing village on Skagit Bay, about an hour's drive north of Yarrow Heights. My mother's grandfather had a small, single-room house there, known in the Connor family as "the cabin." A few years ago, Mom took Samantha and me up for a weekend, while Dad was covering the World Series in New York. I had a good memory of Skagit Harbor and wondered why we'd never gone back.

Dad hadn't liked it, I guess. He thought Skagit Harbor was funky and boring. The kinds of people who lived there tended to be pretty ordinary, with what Dad called a "hippie infiltration." He meant artists who made their living doing carpentry or waiting on tables in restaurants, marginal people in his opinion.

I was taken by surprise. "The cabin? What about it?"

"Well. I've gone up a few times this spring. I've been repainting it, fixing things up. Clearing away the underbrush. It's like a jungle." Mom paused, smiling faintly. There was some meaning here I wasn't getting, not quite yet. "I'm going to be taking some of my studio things up this weekend. Your father will be away, and . . . I'm wondering if you'd like to come with me. I'll be driving back Sunday night."

Suddenly I was on my feet. I was furious, and frightened.

"Mom, why are you provoking him? Why are you doing this?"

Mom stared at me. She'd been touching the scarf, making sure it hadn't slipped around. I could see the faint lines in her face, and the metallic-gray cobwebby streaks in her hair.

"P-provoke? What do you mean, Francesca?"

"Mother, you know exactly what I mean."

"Your—father? You think I'm provoking your father?"

"Aren't you?"

"Francesca, this is out of your depth. This isn't a topic I care to discuss with you."

cuff (n) end of a shirt sleeve at the wrist **rim** (n) *(Augen) ränder* **funky** (adj.) AE (sl.) stinking, smelly **underbrush** AE (BE undergrowth) bushes and small trees growing under or around bigger trees **to be out of sb.'s depth** to be too difficult for sb. to understand

Mom was on her feet now, too. I would remember how weird this was: there was actual fear in her face.

I said, on the verge of tears, "Look, you just asked me, Mother, didn't you? 'What's wrong, Francesca?' So I'm telling you what I think is wrong. You're doing things to deliberately make Daddy angry. You know how he is, and you keep doing them." My voice was choked. I could hardly breathe. It was like I'd dived into the water but couldn't swim back to the surface—something was dragging at my ankles.

Mom said, stammering, "Francesca, you don't understand. It's—complicated." She seemed confused. She had a new, nervous habit of turning a ring on her finger, a chunky silver ring in the shape of a dove she'd brought back from Santa Barbara, made by the same Navajo silversmith who'd made my ponytail clasp.

I said, "If you provoke Dad, he'll react. That's his personality."

"But—don't you think that I have a 'personality,' too?"

"No. I mean, not like Dad. He can't help it, and you can."

"Your father and I love each other, honey. Very much. And we love you. But our values are different now. I—I feel differently about things. I want to live, before it's too late."

"'Live'? Why can't you live here, like you always did? Why are things different now? Samantha is scared you and Daddy are going to get a divorce. Half the kids in her class have parents who are getting divorced."

"Samantha thinks—that? Has she said so?"

"No. She hasn't said so. Not in so many words."

"Have you been talking about this with her? You haven't been frightening her, have you, Francesca?" Mom's voice was shaking.

"No. You're the one who's frightening her. You're frightening me. You seem so—" My face was burning. I had to bite my lip to keep from screaming. "— *unconscious*. Like you're sleepwalking or something. You don't know the effect you're having on Daddy."

Mom chose her words carefully. I would wonder later if they'd been rehearsed.

"Francesca, honey—I mean, Franky—you know nothing about this, really. I'm so sorry that you've been anxious, and that Samantha has been anxious, but"—she was trying to smile, but the staples had all come out, and the smile was like a fish's grimace, and her eyes were bloodshot and scared as if Dad was standing just outside the room about to rush in—

chunky heavy, solid **to rehearse** to prepare **staple** (n) here: allusion to the smile fastened to her face by "staples" *(Heftklammern)*

"your father and I have discussed it at length. He understands that I'd like a little more time alone— away from Seattle, mainly. Not away from my family, but—away from Seattle. Away from this house. He has said I can fix up the cabin in Skagit Harbor, and I can spend time there. Of course, not permanently. I'd always be coming back, every few days. Your father has said so."

This was a surprise. I hadn't expected this.

"He has? Dad has?"

"And there's no talk of divorce, dear. If Samantha ever speaks of such a thing, Franky, please tell her: there is no talk of your father and me getting a divorce, now or ever."

It was strange, how Mom uttered these words. *Now or ever.* Like they weren't hers but someone else's.

Mom turned, wiping at her eyes, and left my room. I wanted to call her back. I wanted to hug her, and feel her arms around me. At the same time, I wanted her gone; I couldn't bear looking at that smile any longer, or the fading plum-colored bruise just visible beneath her jaw.

***

Hi Todd.

Sorry to bother you (again).

Did you know, Mom is fixing up the cabin in Skagit Harbor, & she'll be going up there sometimes? She just told me.

But NO DIVORCE she says. NOW OR EVER.

I guess this is good news. (Isn't it?)

I mean, the way they've been. Since last winter. Let me know what you think, or what you know.

(Are you in contact with Dad?)

Hope things are OK there at Pullman.

Franky

Todd never replied. Actually, I'd thought this time he would.

to fix sth. up to decorate or repair a room etc.

FIVE
"separated": june

Except they weren't.

It was never like people thought.

The Pierson family was not *breaking up*.

Dad explained to Samantha and me. Taking our hands in his hands, and speaking matter-of-factly but gently: "Your mother is in her own zone, girls. More and more, that's where you'll find her."

Mom was away for two days in a row. Then she returned, and next time she was away for three days. She took Rabbit with her in the station wagon. The house was strange and sad and lonely without them. Almost you could hear the echoes of voices, and of Rabbit's little panting yips. *In her own zone. More and more. Where you'll find her.*

It felt wrong, to return from school and Mom wasn't there. You couldn't help but think bad things.

Samantha said, "Franky, doesn't Mom love us anymore?"

"Ask her. How would I know?"

"Sometimes I hate her!" Samantha's small face crinkled with an impish defiance. "I don't care if she ever comes home.

Later, Samantha said, worriedly, "Franky? What if Mom doesn't ever come home?"

"Don't be silly. Mom is coming home day after tomorrow."

"She is?"

"You know she is." I pretended to be exasperated with my dazed little sister.

Samantha smiled, poking her thumb at her mouth. "Oh, well. I guess I did. But I forgot."

***

We didn't miss her! We went to school like always. We had our friends. We had our school activities that mean so much when you're involved in them, though afterward you'll hardly remember why. It felt good to be out of the house and at Forrester, where I was a lanky, red-haired, pony-

station wagon AE (BE estate car) *Kombiwagen* **yip** (n) AE (inf.) yelp **to crinkle** *sich in Falten legen* **impish** naughty, mischievous **defiance** resistance, opposition **dazed** confused, bewildered **lanky** tall, slender

tailed sophomore who had a quick, just-slightly-scratchy-sounding laugh and never gave the impression of taking myself too seriously. "Franky, what's up?" friends would call out to me, swinging along the corridors between classes. I was numb much of the time like I'd been injected with novocaine. In lavatory mirrors I'd catch myself smiling Mom's cheery sta-pled-on smile.

People like you when you're upbeat, a little rowdy, unpredictable. They don't like you when you mope.

Dad began saying to Samantha and me, "You know, nobody likes girls who mope."

You know, Franky's going through this thing.

What thing?

Her mom and dad.

I wasn't sure if I heard this, exactly. At Forrester. In the locker room, before our last swim meet of the season.

No, what? That's why she's been so spaced out?

At Forrester, I was on the yearbook committee, and I belonged to the Drama Club and the Girls' Sports Club. Although I wasn't one of the stars on the swim team, I had my isolated, unexpected moments when I swam like a suddenly crazed/demonic fish. *Freaky Green Eyes racing for her life.* I helped our team win a crucial meet, but I wasn't big enough or strong enough or good enough to be consistent, which means reliable. Yet Meg Tyler, our swim coach, was sympathetic with me, and had a way of taking me aside as if I was someone special, or should have been. At the last meet, which Forrester won, if just barely, she said, "Franky, good work! Next year you're going to come into your own, I predict."

Next year, I hope I'll be here.

I told Miss Tyler thanks. I told her she was a terrific coach. I was touched by her faith in me though I didn't believe it for a nanosecond.

Faster and faster the days went. Everybody was looking forward to summer. I tried to feel that way, too. I stayed up late finishing papers for English and social studies that were overdue, telling myself *Freaky can*

sophomore (n) AE student in the second year of a course at a college or university **novocaine** (n) local anaesthetic **upbeat** (adj.) optimistic, cheerful **to mope** to be gloomy, sad **locker room** AE changing room with lockers *(Spinden)* **spaced out** (inf.) here: lost on thought, absent-minded **consistent** steady **to be sympathetic with sb.** to care and feel sorry about sb.'s problems **overdue** (adj.) unfinished by the time expected

handle this. Like a tricky dive: take it slow. Studying for exams, cramming my head so it felt almost good. With Mom not home much, I could stay up half the night and nobody would know. (Dad was often out. He'd come back around two A.M. some nights.) I took my exams, walked out of school with my mind wiped blank like a blackboard.

I did okay. I didn't fail any subject. Actually I raised my grade in honors English to A–, where I'd been dragging along with Bs and incompletes all semester. Samantha did okay, too. Finished fifth grade with all As and a single B (gym). I was proud of her, and I hoped that Mom and Dad were, too.

***

"When can we come with you, Mom?" Samantha kept asking. And Mom would say, "When your school is out." But when school was out, and Samantha asked, Mom said evasively, with a nervous flutter of her eyelids, "When I'm finished painting the cabin. When your father thinks it's appropriate."

Samantha said, jabbing her thumb at her mouth, "Franky and I can help you paint, Mom. You let us last time. You said we painted your studio really well."

"Yes, honey. You certainly did. But . . ." Mom paused. For a moment she seemed confused, as if she couldn't remember what she was supposed to be saying. ". . . it's another time now, honey."

I wanted to ask her what painting her cabin had to do with Dad's opinion. And how long was it taking to paint her cabin, which was the size of a single room? But resentment for this woman was like a big clump of hot dough in my throat.

Go away then. Stay away.

You don't love us. You love the "zone" you're in.

***

honors AE (pl.) a course of study in a subject of a higher or more specialized character, *etwa: Leistungskurs* **incompletes** (n) *mangelhafte Noten* **evasive** not willing to answer a question directly **to jab** to push sth. towards sth./sb. with a short quick movement **dough** [dou] (n) *Teig*

As soon as the station wagon pulled out of the driveway, know what I did? I made certain my cell phone was turned off.

For hours each day, except when Maria was here (Maria was the Filipino woman Mom had hired to oversee the household in her absence), I kept the family phone off the hook, too. Mom called home at least twice a day; she could leave a message in our voice mail.

So I wouldn't be waiting for the phones to ring every minute I was home.

I stopped bringing my friends home. With Mom away, the house was deadly quiet like a museum nobody ever visits. Even Maria banging around vacuuming the big rooms overhead (that didn't need vacuuming, but Maria had to do something to earn her salary) was a kind of dead absence of sound. Rabbit's nervous high-pitched yipping, which Dad disliked, I kept imagining I heard, but at a distance, as if Rabbit was somewhere in the neighborhood, lost. Samantha and I kept thinking we saw him in the kitchen by his food and water dishes. We heard his toenails clicking on the tile floor, and his eager panting breath.

Samantha said, "It isn't fair, Franky, is it? Rabbit is our dog, too."

"I guess Mom isn't thinking of us right now. 'She's in her own zone.'" I spoke lightly, not sarcastically.

Samantha asked, "What's a 'zone,' Franky? Daddy didn't say."

"Her own space, like. In her own head. Doing what she wants to do, not what other people want her to do. I guess."

In fact, I didn't know. But I knew I hated that zone.

Pretty soon we figured out the schedule: Mom was gone two or three days a week, and most of this time Dad was home. (When he wasn't traveling, he worked in downtown Seattle. He covered local sports events when they "impacted" on the national scene.) The day after Mom returned, Dad would leave. There was always some overlap. A family meal together, an evening. Samantha was nervous a lot, not knowing what was going on, exactly; I tried to be neutral. I guess I was stiff with Mom, feeling she was betraying us. With Dad, when all he wanted was his "good girls" laughing at his jokes, it wasn't so hard.

I wondered: did Mom and Dad sleep together any longer? In the same bed?

cell(ular) phone AE mobile phone **bang around** move around a place making a lot of noise **to impact on sth.** to affect, have an effect on **overlap** (n) here: period of time when both parents were together

It was weird—some nights at dinner they got along really well. Called each other "honey" and "darling" and were extra nice. Then, next day, Dad would be flying out to Miami, Chicago, Austin. And when he returned, it would be time for Mom to pack up her things, kiss us good-bye, call, "Rabbit! C'mon, boy," and drive off in the station wagon to Skagit Harbor. Once Samantha stood in the driveway yelling after Mom, "It isn't fair, it isn't! Rabbit is our dog, too."

***

Sometimes when Mom was gone, the house was suddenly noisy upstairs and out on the redwood deck. Dad was "having friends over for drinks." They'd arrive around six P.M., and around nine P.M. they'd leave for dinner in one of the trendy Seattle restaurants Dad took Samantha and me to sometimes. On his way out of the house, Dad always came to see us downstairs to inform us he was "going out for a bite to eat" with his friends, and not to wait up for him.

Samantha would say primly, "Daddy, you already ate with *us*."

Increasingly, a woman unknown to us would be hanging on to Dad's arm and would want to say "hi!" and "good night" to Dad's daughters. (Samantha camped out in my room until she went to bed next door in her own room. She wasn't too much of a nuisance, except if I was talking with friends on the phone; I didn't like her listening and butting in.) Samantha thought this woman was always the same person, but I knew there was more than one woman. It was easy to confuse them because they were all blond, glamorous, and years younger than Mom. They looked like TV news or weather girls. They looked like models. Dad never introduced them to us; maybe he didn't remember their names. He'd knock on my door, push it open even as I called out, "Come in," and he'd come inside just a few steps, and the blond woman would be beside him, but just slightly behind him, and he'd say proudly, "See? My good girls. Sam-Sam, the little one, and Franky, who's a star swimmer at Forrester Academy. Terrific, aren't they?" The blond woman would gaze earnestly at Samantha and me as if we were specimens of some rare unnamed species, and she'd squeeze Dad's upper arm through his sports shirt and say breathily, "Oh Reid, gosh, *yes*. They take after their *daddy*."

primly (adv.) in a formal tone **nuisance** ['nju:sns] source of annoyance **to butt in** to interrupt **terrific** (inf.) wonderful, excellent **specimen(s)** sample(s) **species** ['spi:ʃi:z] *Art, Gattung*

Once, Freaky Green Eyes intruded. Saying, "Actually, we take after our mom, too. Have you met Mom?"

The look Dad flashed me, even as he smiled, and laughed!

Saying his usual, "Okay, girls. Don't wait up for your old dad."

Samantha was okay, I guess. Learning to adjust to the New Schedule. I felt sorry for her. I could see she was crying in secret, because she knew that crying annoyed Dad; and sometimes, I have to admit, I got impatient with her, too. (Seeing Samantha cry made me want to cry. No thanks!)

Samantha had friends from her school, but they didn't live close by us, so when Mom wasn't here to drive her, she was sort of stuck at home. She was lonely, and emotional. Just to get attention, sometimes, five or six times a day she'd ask if Mom had called, if I'd checked our voice mail. Actually coming into my room in the middle of the night—when I'd finally fallen asleep—pleading, "Franky? Did you doublecheck the messages for tonight?"

Of course, we could call Mom. But Mom rarely answered her phone, and she didn't have voice mail. I asked her why, and she said evasively, "Phones make me nervous. You never know who might be calling."

Mom wasn't an e-mail person, either. She said computers made her nervous, so she didn't take her laptop to Skagit Harbor.

And Dad, too. Often he was out of reach. Sometimes an assistant would call. "Francesca Pierson? Hold for Reid Pierson." After a long wait, and a series of clicks, Dad's voice would come on the phone, loud in my ear and sounding harassed. "Hi there, sweetie. What's up?" Somehow, wherever Dad was in the country, he had the idea I'd called him.

"But Dad, you called *me*."

"I did?" Dad sounded vague, bemused. He'd laugh, as if a third party had played a joke on us both, and Reid Pierson was too good a sport to take offense. "Well. Just saying hello, honey. Is your mother anywhere near?"

If I said yes, Dad would say quickly, "No-no, Franky. I don't need to speak with her. Just checking, see?"

After Dad broke the connection, I'd stand holding the receiver to my ear like a hypnotized person, waiting for a voice to return.

Then in June, my mother's older sister, Aunt Vicky, who was my favorite of all the Connor/Pierson relatives, began e-mailing me. Aunt Vicky had

to intrude to interfere with, disturb **harassed** under stress **bemused** confused

called me four or five times and I guess I'd never called her back, for some reason.

(Maybe I didn't want Aunt Vicky to hear something weak and frightened in my voice. She was sharp and picked up on things that even Mom didn't.)

Hi there Franky:

Just checking in. I miss you. Let's plan a winter trip. I'm thinking of Costa Rica.

Right now, I'm wondering how you and Samantha are. Give me a call tomorrow, will you? Thanks.
Love & kisses,
Aunt Vicky

Well, I didn't. I resented Aunt Vicky butting in.

Wondering what Mom had told her. Wondering if there was some secret about my mother and father that Aunt Vicky knew and I didn't.

Dear Franky,

I'm a little concerned, you don't answer your telephone calls & you don't answer e-mail. Shall I drive up? This weekend?

Love & kisses,
You-Know-Who

Quickly I typed out:

Dear Aunt Vicky,

Samantha & I are fine. Things are fine here.
We're out of school till Sept.

I stared at the computer screen for five, ten minutes. . . . Finally I added:

Please just leave us alone, Aunt Vicky.

Love,
Franky

(Why was I so angry with Aunt Vicky? Actually, I loved Aunt Vicky. We got along really well together, liked the same kind of jokes, liked swimming and the outdoors. Aunt Vicky had taken me lots of places including, when I was twelve, on an unforgettable trip to the mountains of northern Mexico to observe the monarch butterfly migration. She was crazy about Samantha, too.)

I never clicked Send, though. After a while deliberating, I clicked Delete.

There was this puppet-girl Franky Pierson. I hoped that people were marveling how extra normal and totally sane she was.

For instance: I helped Jenn Carpenter's mother organize a surprise sixteenth birthday party for Jenn on June 20, which was the eve of her birthday. For weeks we made plans by telephone and e-mail. (During which time, when Mrs Carpenter asked about my mother, I told her always cheerfully that Mom was "fine"—Mom was "working at her art.") Twyla and I were entrusted to pretend to be dropping by the Carpenters' to pick Jenn up for a movie, but when Jenn walked into the Carpenters' family room, where we were waiting, there were twentythree of Jenn's friends plus relatives and even Jenn's father, who'd flown home early from a business conference in Rio. When we started singing "Happy Birthday," Jenn gaped at us wide-eyed. Her jaw literally dropped. So funny! Mrs Carpenter was videotaping. There were balloons, there were mounds of presents. Someone put a glittery hat on Jenn's head. We laughed and laughed. I wiped at my eyes seeing how totally surprised and happy Jenn was, how people loved her and she loved them.

The thought came to me *I wish I was that young.*

"Francesca? It's me."

After a while it got to be that, when Mom came home, sometimes I wasn't home. And if I was, sometimes I didn't come out of my room to meet her. Stayed at my computer cruising the Web. Clicking onto sites that took me to distant places. (I was getting interested in paleontology. Paleontology digs in Montana, Wyoming. Digging up bones from one hundred million years ago. In some clear, dry climate where you could see for miles, where it wasn't always misty or raining.) I'd hear the station wagon in the driveway, and Samantha running, and Rabbit barking, and I knew that Mom would be wondering where I was, waiting for me to come out and hug her. I thought, *Let her wait. Let her wonder.*

migration movement from one place to another to live (resp. work) there **to deliberate** to think about **to delete** to remove, cross out **to entrust sb. to do sth.** to ask sb. to do sth. **to cruise the Web** *im Internet surfen*

Soon, then, Dad would depart. And when Dad returned, Mom would leave again for Skagit Harbor. Lots of people in this part of the state commute, by ferry as well as car, so I tried to think of Mom and Dad as perpetual commuters. What was strange was that Skagit Harbor was so close to Yarrow Heights, actually; an hour's drive along Route 5 north skirting the foothills of the Cascade Mountains. Samantha kept saying to Mom, "Why can't we go with you? You promised!" And Mom turned the silver ring around her finger nervously, and said, "Honey, I did promise. I haven't forgotten. But this isn't the right time." Samantha said loudly, "When, then?" and Mom said, "When your father says so."

Another time, Samantha said slyly, "Mom? Daddy is away until Friday. We could go with you to the cabin, and you could bring us back before Daddy came home. He wouldn't know!" I saw Mom glance at me, her worried, frightened eyes, and I knew she was hoping I wouldn't think that this was a great idea, too. I hated seeing her so scared seeming and weak. I guess my face hardened, and my eyes. Mom said, "Samantha, no. That wouldn't be a good idea at all. Your father would be furious with us. All of us."

But when Samantha asked Dad when we could visit Mom, Dad said with an air of surprise, "Sweetie, it isn't up to me. It's up to her."

(Lately, Dad spoke of Mom as "her" or "she." He never said "your mother" or "Krista" any longer.)

Samantha protested, "But Daddy, Mommy says it's up to you. Mommy says to ask *you*."

"No. She's just pretending that. It isn't so."

Confused by this, Samantha stood blinking. She had the look of a child abandoned on the median of an expressway, as traffic sped past in both directions.

"Dad*dy*! Can we all drive up to Mommy's cabin, just for a little while? I want to see Mommy's cabin!" Samantha's voice was shrill, and I knew it was a mistake but there was no way to stop her. She kept on like this, whining, childish, pulling at Dad's arm until he lost patience and took hold of her wrist and twisted it, and Samantha whimpered like an injured puppy, and

to commute to travel to and from work **to skirt** to move round **Cascade Mountains** part of the Cascade Range, a major mountain range of western North America. It extends from southern British Columbia through Washington and Oregon to Northern California **sly** (adj.) cunning, clever **to blink** to shut and open the eyes quickly **median** (n) AE strip of land that separates the two sides of a motorway **expressway** AE motorway **to whimper** to make a low crying sound esp. with fear or pain

dropped to one knee, and Dad released her, breathing hard, saying in a level, calm voice, "I told you, Samantha. I'm not going to tell you again. Both of you had better get this straight. It's up to *her*. Not *me*."

Samantha bit her lower lip to keep from crying. She knew she'd better not.

By the time we went to bed that night, Samantha's wrist was circled in red welts from where Dad's fingers had twisted. Next morning, it looked as if Samantha was wearing a bracelet of plum-colored bruises.

I felt sorry for Samantha but, well—she'd provoked Dad. She would have to learn not to do that.

As I'd learned, at about her age.

It wasn't until two days later that Mom noticed Samantha's wrist. It wasn't until two days later that Mom was home, to notice anything.

Mom said, "Samantha, what's that? What happened to your wrist?" and Samantha murmured, "I don't know, maybe I . . . fell down, I guess."

"Fell down—where?" Mom asked, concerned, and Samantha shrugged away from her, not wanting Mom to touch her. She said contemptuously, "Where's anybody fall? On the dumb *ground*."

This was June.

June was a long month.

I'd been supposed to spend two weeks at the Bainbridge Island Arts Camp, where some friends of mine from school were going, but I never got around to filling out the application, and Mom must have forgotten, too. Every week Dad was promising we'd go away for a few days to Cape Flattery, where some rich Seattle businessman had a place on the ocean, but (somehow I knew this) Dad was embarrassed to accept an invitation without his wife; how could he explain his wife's absence, unless Krista could be talked into joining her family. (I overheard certain phone calls. I wasn't eavesdropping, but I overheard.) But so many people wanted Reid Pierson to stay with them at their beautiful summer places, how could he choose? And it was baseball season. And Maria was fired (by Dad, for no reason we ever learned), so another woman had to be hired. And Samantha came down with summer bronchitis. And that was June.

bracelet band worn around one's wrist as a decoration **dumb** (adj.) AE stupid **Bainbridge Island** island in Puget Sound known for its natural beauty **Cape Flattery** the northwesternmost point of the USA **to overhear** accidentally hear what people say when they do not know that you hear them **to eavesdrop** deliberately listen to other people's conversations

SIX
cape flattery: july 4

"We can have a good time, Franky, can't we? Even if Mom isn't with us?"

For Fourth of July Dad finally drove us out to Cape Flattery, which is about as far west and north on the Olympic Peninsula as you can get. We were excited! It was the first outing we'd had with our father in a long time. The Blounts' lodge, as it was called, was six miles south of the Cape, built on a high, rocky bluff overlooking the white-capped greenish waves of the Pacific Ocean. We'd be going sailing and whale watching, Dad promised. The Blounts had three children, two boys and a girl, so we'd have someone to "relate to."

There'd been the possibility of Mom joining us for the long weekend. At least, that was what Dad hinted. Except on the morning we left for Cape Flattery, Dad told us there'd been a sudden change of plans. "She changed her mind, girls. She just called and said she wasn't coming." Samantha cried, "Why? Why isn't Mom coming?" and Dad said, shrugging, "Sweetie, you'll have to ask her."

Later Dad said, in a voice meant to be forgiving, "Like I said, girls, she's in her own zone now. 'Skagit Harbor.'"

Each time Dad spoke of Mom, his words seemed to take on newer and more mysterious meanings.

(First they swear to you there's "nobody else." Then, later, you learn that not only is there "sombody else," it's this "somebody else" who's the reason for the weird behavior: quarreling, crying, shoving-around, falling-down-drunk stuff that makes you ashamed you even know these people, let alone they're your parents. And sure, there's a divorce. And it drags on, and on. And it never ends, because it's inside you, too. And you carry it with you wherever you go, like a turtle with a crooked shell.

This is what friends of mine have said. Girls at Forrester whose parents went through divorce. I'd hear, and I'd think, *But not the Piersons. We're special.*)

Olympic Peninsula arm of land in the western part of the state of Washington limited on the west by the Pacific, on the north by the Strait of Juan de Fuca, and on the east by Puget Sound **bluff** (n) here: cliff **relate to sb.** here: identify with sb. **to shove around** *schikanieren* **let alone** without considering **turtle** reptile with a soft body protected by a hard shell, *Schildkröte* **crooked** (adj.) ['krukid] deformed, misshapen

Samantha's bruise bracelet was mostly faded now. You had to know what it was to notice it. On the drive to Cape Flattery, Samantha in the front seat of the car with Dad while I sat in the back, sprawled out, reading and scribbling in my diary, I'd see Samantha examine her wrist now and then, lifting her slender arm to the light.

Since Dad had disciplined her, Samantha was better behaved in his presence. I guess I was, too.

When we got to the Blounts' lodge, it was midafternoon. Dad had trouble locating the property, it was set back so far from the road in a dense evergreen forest. He'd been telling us about the Blounts, who were strong supporters of his and loyal friends. Mr. Blount was a multimillionaire, and he was locally famous for his generous donations to civic causes and charities. As a distinguished alum of the U. of Washington he'd endowed athletic scholarships for both men and women, including, just last year, a scholarship in Dad's name: the Reid Pierson Class of '78 Football Scholarship. Dad marveled, "That was one of the great honors of my life, I can tell you. It was an absolute surprise."

When Dad spoke like this, I couldn't tell if he was addressing just Samantha and me or other, invisible listeners. Sometimes I could almost see this audience, on the far side of blinding lights. I could hear their cheers and applause.

Finally Dad found the Blounts' driveway. Bumpy, bouncy, you needed a Jeep to navigate it. Dad was cursing under his breath, and Samantha and I were very quiet. But there was a clearing after a quarter mile, sunlight flooded in, and the Blounts' lodge lifted above us, so impressive we just stared. Dad murmured happily, "Now there's class, girls. Wealth and taste." The "lodge" was the size of a small hotel, made of redwood logs and stone, with numerous sliding doors, balconies, and open decks. There were beautiful stone chimneys and what appeared to be Indian gargoyles and totem poles used for decorative purposes. Beyond the house was the bluff, and an enormous sweeping view of the ocean. For once the mist wasn't obscuring the horizon.

to sprawl out to stretch out **lodge** (n) cottage **donation** money you give to sb. or an organization so as to help them **alum** (n) AE (inf.) former student of a school, college, etc. **to endow** to finance, give money for **to curse under one's breath** to swear in a quiet voice so that nobody can hear you **clearing** (n) small area in a forest where there are no trees **gargoyle** (n) *Wasserspeier* **sweeping** extensive, wide

There were at least eight vehicles in the Blounts' horseshoe driveway. My heart sank—I hadn't anticipated so many Fourth of July guests. Somehow from the way Dad had talked, it had seemed as if Reid Pierson and his family would be the only guests.

Dad was in a great mood immediately. Shaking hands, kissing cheeks, and hugging. Everybody knew Reid Pierson, and everybody was drawn to Reid Pierson. From time to time Dad would remember that Samantha and I had come with him, and he'd wave us over, or snap his fingers like a magician, "Girls! Sam-Sam and Franky, c'mere." For Dad was proud of his daughters, he wanted everyone to know.

Samantha was an honor student at Country Day. Franky was a star swimmer and diver on the girls' team at Forrester. Todd, who hadn't been able to join us today, was into serious football at Washington State.

When Dad was asked about his wife, he smiled and shook his head wryly. "Krista sends her regrets. She's so terribly sorry not to be with us. She has an extremely dependent family down in Portland; they're forever calling upon her to help them with 'crises' . . ."

For a moment I wondered: Is this true? Mom isn't in Skagit Harbor, but in Portland? Maybe that was why Aunt Vicky had called and e-mailed me?

As soon as I saw the Blounts, especially Mrs Blount, who was about Mom's age but sleekly blond and glamorous in that way Mom no longer wanted to be, I was lonely for home, and for Mom. In this beautiful place on the ocean, on the Fourth of July. I felt lonely, gawky, self-conscious. Samantha and I were like orphans at this house party where everybody knew everybody else and there were children running in and out and strangers carrying drinks drifting by, crying, "Happy Fourth! Great weather, isn't it? For once." A witty variant of this was "Great weather, isn't it? Bud ordered it."

Mrs Blount seized both my hands in hers and said, "Franky, is it? I'm sooo sorry your mother wasn't able to join us. I hope the 'family crisis' isn't terribly serious?"

horseshoe driveway *hufeisenförmige Auffahrt* **Fourth of July** Independence Day **honor student** student in a US elementary, middle or high school respected for his/her excellent achievements at school **c'mere** come here **Country Day (School)** US type of school based on the Country Day School movement of the early 20th century. These schools aiming at character formation were originally built outside the cities, in the "country" (i.e. the suburbs where the wealthy people live), in order to protect the students from the problems of the industrial cities **to be into sth.** be fond of, interested in sth. **Washington State** here: WSU **sleek** (adj.) smooth and shining **gawky** awkward **orphan** (n) child whose parents are dead

"Just some people dying, maybe."

This was a Freaky remark—I couldn't resist. The look on Mrs Blount's tight, manicured face!

"Oh, dear. I hope—it isn't—" Still, Mrs Blount meant to be upbeat at her party and needed my help; we were clumsy as canoers struggling with outsize paddles, about to capsize.

I mumbled a vague reply that might have been interpreted as *It's okay, it won't last much longer*, and Mrs Blount pretended to feel relief hearing this, and smiled at me and squeezed my hands in a gesture of maternal sympathy. But her gaze slipped past my head to fasten eagerly upon another, more promising guest who'd just arrived.

"Excuse me, dear! We'll catch up later."

There came our host, Bud Blount, to say hello to me. He was a hearty, red-faced man of about fifty with thick graying hair on his head and a darker patch of hair at the deep V of his sports shirt. "Your father says you're quite a swimmer, eh? Diver? Me too. I mean, I used to be. In college. C'mere, darlin'." He wanted to show me his Olympic-size pool, which was visible from one end of the redwood deck, but he was distracted by other guests, including my father, who were praising the wine he was serving and asking about its vintage. I would have slipped away while they were talking, but Mr Blount had hold of my arm. He said, "My sixteen-year-old, Sean, is a helluva diver too. Sean? Where's Sean, Leila? Tell you what, I'm going to propose that you two sexy kids change into swimsuits and put on a little performance for us, eh? I bet you're terrific. *My* diving days are over." He chuckled, patting his hard-looking stomach that protruded over the belt of his khaki shorts. "All I can do now are belly flops, but kids like you, you're in terrific shape." Mr Blount not only tugged my ponytail fondly, like I was five years old, but made a playful swipe as if to pinch my bare midriff.

Hey! I didn't like this. But it happened fast, and Mr Blount was obviously not a bad guy, just gregarious and trying to be funny the way Dad was sometimes when he'd been drinking. So I resisted the impulse to push away from him. I gave him the excuse that I wasn't "swimming or diving right now"—it was "that time for me." This was a Freaky trick: acting like I was really really embarrassed, and causing Mr Blount to be embar-

upbeat (adj.) cheerful **clumsy** awkward **to capsize** to overturn, *kentern* **vintage** particular year or place in which a wine is produced, or the wine itself **helluva** (sl.) 'hell of a' here: terrific, excellent **to chuckle** to laugh quietly **to protrude** to stick out **belly flop** (inf.) *Bauchklatscher* **swipe** (n) strike **midriff** *Taille* **gregarious** company-loving

rassed, too, after he caught on. His heavy face was flushing a deeper shade of pink. He mumbled, "Well. I'm—sorry."

"Some other time, maybe. Invite us back."

Samantha and I had a nice bunk-bed girls' room on the second floor of the lodge, and Dad's room was just across the way. It seemed strange to be in a place like this, like a hotel, without Mom close by to supervise us. Samantha whispered, "We could call her, Franky, couldn't we? Just to say hello." But the cell phone was mine, and I vetoed the idea.

I didn't bother unpacking most of my things. Left them in the suitcase. We were staying only three nights.

There was to be an outdoor barbecue, a suckling pig roasted on a spit. The smell of roasting flesh permeated the air and was both mouthwatering and sickening. (Twyla was a vegetarian. I was fully intending to become a vegetarian, too, except I knew Dad would be annoyed: he called it a "hippie affectation.") I was feeling more and more Freaky-restless, wondering why I was here. Wondering why I hadn't had the courage to tell Dad I'd prefer to spend the Fourth of July in Skagit Harbor with Mom.

You wouldn't, ever. You don't have that courage.

Know what you are? A hypocrite.

Freaky's derisive voice in my head.

Before the barbecue, while it was still daylight, Mr Blount took some of his guests out on his fortyfoot sailing yacht *Triumph II* to look for whales. I was excited about going—I loved those smallish killer whales that relate so strangely to human beings—but the air was cold on the water; the wind blew spray into our faces, and the season was no longer summer but felt more like November. And Samantha was frightened of the way the boat bounced and bucked sideways against the waves.

Mr Blount was at the helm, and Dad was his cocaptain. The two men were laughing and shouting, "Whale! Whale ahoy! To the starboard, keep your eyes open." We kept our eyes open but didn't see any whales; or, if we saw them, we didn't know what we were seeing in the roiling water because they surfaced and sank again in nearly the same motion. I wondered if the whales were teasing us, laughing at us. After about fifteen minutes Samantha's lips and fingernails were turning blue and she was

to catch on to understand, get it **bunk-bed** two single beds fixed one above the other **to veto** to reject **suckling pig** a very young pig **affectation** here: snobbery **derisive** mocking **to bounce** to move up and down **to buck** to move to and fro, up and down in an uncontrolled way **at the helm** at the wheel, in charge **starboard** *Steuerbord* **roiling** (adj.) turbulent, agitated

shivering so badly, I hunted up a sweater for her in the cabin and wrapped it around her. Samantha tried gamely to see what Dad was pointing at, but she was dazed and vacant eyed. The boat dipped and heaved, rocked and rolled. The wind sucked our breaths away. I couldn't even see the Blounts' lodge above the bluff, there was so much spray and mist. But the mood on *Triumph II* was mostly festive, since the adults had been drinking. This was a party after all. Fourth of July.

The Blount brothers, Sean and Chris, had come with us. Sean was a familiar high school type: one of those guys who look slantwise at you like they're assessing you, maybe liking what they see, but maybe not. Ever since we'd been introduced up at the house, Sean seemed undecided about me, impressed that I was Reid Pierson's daughter but unconvinced that I was pretty enough, or sexy enough, for him to waste time on. I was only a year younger than Sean, but probably he thought I was even younger. Still, he seemed to like me. He wanted to impress me. He had a pair of binoculars for me to look through, to see whales in the distance, surfacing and leaping up to flash their sleek, glistening faces in the air, then disappearing again. "See? They're cool, whales." I thanked Sean and handed the binoculars to Samantha.

Sean said he wished they could hunt whales like in *Moby-Dick*. With harpoons. "Know what I'd like to do someday? Catch a baby whale in a net and train it in our pool. And videotape it."

I wondered, could this guy be serious? He seemed to be.

"That's illegal, isn't it?"

Sean grinned and shrugged. "Who's to know? The Coast Guard? The FBI?"

After thirty minutes of bucking the waves, Mr Blount turned the boat around and we headed back to his dock, where the sweet-sickening odor of roasting pig greeted us.

The adults returned to the party on the redwood deck, but Sean had something to show me, his "private zoo." It was a hike uphill from the dock to a grassy area behind the Blounts' three-car garage, where Sean and Chris had a number of cages. Samantha and I were quiet, seeing the brothers' collection of animals: a hare, a fox cub, two nervous raccoons,

to hunt sth. up to search for sth. that is difficult to find **vacant** empty **to dip** to sink **to heave** to rise **to suck sb.'s breath away** take sb.'s breath away **to look slantwise at sb.** to look at sb. out of the corner of one's eye **to assess sb./sth.** to form an opinion of sb./sth., *jem. taxieren* **binoculars** *Fernglas* **odor** (n) smell **fox cub** young fox **raccoon** *Waschbär*

and a young owl. "Pretty cool, huh?" Sean boasted. "The fox especially. The mother comes around, making these barking, mewing noises." He laughed. "If she doesn't watch out, we'll catch her, too. See this trap?"

At least it was a Havahart trap, not a leg-iron trap.

A feeling like flame passed over me. I was so disgusted! But I managed to speak calmly. "Where'd you get all these?" I asked, as if I was truly impressed.

Sean gestured toward the forest. "Right around here. It's a wildlife refuge, that way. We trapped them. There's thousands of them—it's no big deal. I mean, they're not endangered species or anything."

"What are you going to do with them?"

Sean shrugged. "Who cares? It's cool."

Chris echoed his older brother, grinning. "It's cool."

"Your parents don't care?"

Again, Sean shrugged. "No big deal."

Samantha was staring at the hare. He was much larger than a bunny of the kind you see in pet stores at Easter. He was a beautiful, sad-looking creature with dark moist eyes and a quivering nose and strangely short, collapsed-seeming ears. She said, "Don't you feel sorry for them?"

"Hell, no. We feed them real well."

They didn't, though. The plastic water bowls were almost empty, and not very clean. The cages were dirty. Chris was poking a stick at the raccoons and laughing at their terror. Except one of the raccoons bit the stick and nearly pulled it from Chris's hand. "Hey! Watch it!" Chris scolded. For some reason, this was funny: both brothers laughed. Samantha and I were trying to feed the hare grass, but he was apathetic and shrank from us. Sean spilled some pelletlike dog food into the cages, but none of the creatures ate. The fox cub, which was the size of a full-grown cat, was panting, crouched with his back against the wire enclosure of its cage, staring unblinking at us with tawny eyes. His narrow chest rose and fell rapidly. The owl, too, stared unblinking. *We need help. We need you. Save us!* I thought of how my mom might react. Again that hot, flamy sensation passed over my brain, a freaky feeling that excited me. Samantha was saying worriedly, "They're lonely here

Havahart trap brand name for a live animal cage trap **leg-iron trap** a foothold trap that usually inflicts pain **disgusted** outraged, shocked **refuge** (n) place of shelter **bunny** name for a rabbit **moist** (adj.) here: tearful, watery **quivering** slightly shaking **to shrink from sb.** to move back from sb. because of fear **to spill** to pour **pelletlike** in the form of small balls **tawny** brownish-yellow

just by themselves. I wouldn't want to be in a cage! You should let them out—they could go back home."

Sean said, "Sure. When we feel like it."

I didn't want to arouse their distrust. I asked a few questions sort of politely, like I was impressed, and then we went back up on the deck, where people were beginning to eat from a big buffet.

As soon as it was dark, Mr Blount's fireworks display began. He'd hired somebody from Seattle for it. People were ooohing and aaahing like small children, staring up at the multicolored flaring lights that exploded like stars and pressing their hands over their ears, the noise was so loud. I couldn't find Dad at first, then saw him at the far end of the deck surrounded by admirers. He was in a festive mood, one arm loosely slung around the bare shoulders of a very young woman with dramatically straight blond hair. From time to time he called over to Samantha and me, "Hey girls. Having a good time?" and "Terrific display, eh?"

I remembered the promise *No divorce. Not ever.*

Freaky-quick and shrewd, I slipped away from the party while everybody was gaping at the fireworks.

Immediately I went to our car in the driveway. I knew that Dad kept a flashlight in the glove compartment, and I took this flashlight and crept behind the Blounts' garage to the "private zoo." "Fourth of July! Independence Day! Here you go."

One by one I unlatched the cages. First the raccoons, then the fox cub, then the hare, then the owl. My heart was pounding like crazy. I didn't know if I was scared to death or excited. My hands were shaking. At first, not one of the creatures stirred. They were fearful of me, huddling in their cages. The little fox's eyes glared tawny yellow like reflectors. The hare was visibly quivering. I drew back from the cages and lowered the flashlight. "Go! Go back home! You're free."

Still, no one moved.

In the sky above the Blounts' house the fireworks were bursting and blooming. The ooohs! and ahhhs! were louder, people were drunker. I was so disgusted! If animals could think, what would they think of our species? Capable of such silly, extravagant behavior, but at the same time cruel and selfish. Like the Blount brothers. Cruel because they were selfish and ignorant, behaving as if animals weren't "real"—didn't have feelings just like they did.

display (n) show, spectacle **shrewd** sharp-witted, clever **to huddle** to crowd

At last, the larger raccoon leaped down from his cage and went lumbering frantically toward the woods without a backward glance. The other raccoon was more cautious but followed him. The hare seemed paralyzed, his bulging dark eyes blinking spasmodically, but the fox cub was approaching the opened door of his cage, sniffing as if he suspected a trick. The owl hadn't moved, not a feather. I backed away farther and switched off the flashlight.

"Go on! Go home."

Running back to the Blounts' house, I felt *so happy*.

It was a Freaky Green Eyes rush, like adrenaline.

Next morning when the cry went up from the Blount brothers that someone had sabotaged their private zoo, suspicion fell immediately on me, so I shrugged and admitted it.

"Yes, I did it. I opened the cages."

Everybody stared at me. The Blounts, my father, Samantha.

Looking at me like I was some kind of criminal? I just laughed.

Sean said angrily, "You had no right! Those animals were *ours*."

It's Freaky's strategy to be prepared. I'd been rehearsing what I would say. I stood with my hands on my hips and my chin uplifted and said calmly, "Those animals were not yours—they're wild animals. They did not belong to you."

An ugly scene followed. I didn't expect anybody to congratulate me, but I hadn't expected the Blounts to be so angry. I knew that Sean and Chris would be livid, but I believed that mature persons would react differently, yet they didn't. I could see I'd made a false calculation. Still, I tried to maintain my poise. I said, "I let the animals go because it's illegal to keep wild animals in cages, and it's cruel, and I'm not sorry."

Dad said, "Francesca, apologize to these people. Apologize *now*."

"Dad, I can't. I'm not sorry."

"I told you: apologize. *Now*."

I guess it was that that infuriated Dad. Because I was being Freaky-stubborn saying, "I can't. I won't. I did the right thing, and I'm not sorry."

Dad was getting pretty upset. Mr Blount saw and tried to calm him. "Reid, it's all right. The boys can replenish their zoo—there are plenty more animals in these woods—" but Dad kept interrupting, telling me

to lumber to move in a slow, awkward way **to bulge** to stick out **spasmodically** irregularly **livid** (adj.) (inf.) furious **mature** here: sensible **poise** (n) composure, selfassurance **to replenish** to stock up, replace

to apologize, and I had to shake my head no, I could not, and finally Dad lost control, and grabbed hold of my arm and shook, shook, shook me so hard my teeth rattled in my head. "Damn you. I'm telling you. Apologize to these people, Francesca, or I'll break every bone in your miserable body!"

"Reid, no! Don't—"

"No, Reid—*please*!"

Both the Blounts intervened, alarmed. Mr Blount tugged at my father's fingers until he released me, and I stumbled from the room crying.

Dad drove us back to Yarrow Heights that morning.

Our Fourth of July visit to Cape Flattery came to an abrupt end.

In the car, there were hours of stony silence. Not even the radio or a CD. Samantha, sitting beside Dad in the front, finished one Nancy Drew novel and began another. Only a few times she dared to glance back at her disgraced older sister, who lay on the backseat with a damp cloth over her face, trying not to whimper in pain. My head was pounding, my neck and even my upper spine were thrumming with pain. All I knew was that Freaky had done the right thing, and Freaky had to accept punishment for doing it.

Seeing the raccoons lumber away into the woods. Seeing the hare shaking free of his trance. The fox cub, sniffing and cautious. And the owl with his soft gray feathers and fierce staring gaze at last flying away . . .

Yes, you have to accept punishment sometimes for doing what is right.

SEVEN
shame

Break every bone in your body.

Every bone in your miserable body.

Those nights I woke every hour hearing my father's voice close above me. Sweaty and my heart pumping not in Freaky-elation but in panic. I felt the fingers digging into my arms in hatred of my stubborn flesh. I tasted the shame of that spectacle like something rotted and black in my mouth. And the eyes of others, staring. And my own eyes, staring.

Nancy Drew fictional heroine of a popular mystery/detective series **to pound** to beat **spine** (n) *Wirbelsäule* **to thrum** here: to drum **elation** happiness

It hadn't been the first time. But it was the first time I'd been disciplined before strangers.

Reid, don't. Don't hurt her. Reid . . .

Keep out of this. She has to be disciplined. Look at her—she doesn't even cry.

She's terrified, Reid. She can't cry....

Get the hell away. A fine mothering job you've done.

I woke and couldn't remember. What I remembered was a dream, wasn't it? An ugly dream. And sometimes, though I was conscious, I couldn't move my arms or legs, only my eyes, I could open my eyes and I could see the hazy proportions of the room (but which room was it? Which bed was this?), but I couldn't move, almost I could not breathe. *She doesn't mean it, darling. She's only two. She can't reason or think, darling. She can't help soiling herself if she's scared. She isn't doing it deliberately. She's only two. . . .* I shut my eyes and slept.

Days passed. Dad refused to speak with me.

If we were in the same room together, he looked through me. He made a show of hugging and kissing Samantha, who leaped into his arms. "Daddy! Are you going away *again*?" But of course Dad was going away, to St. Louis. Baseball, a doubleheader. Which meant that Mom would be returning, and Mom did return, arriving with Rabbit in the station wagon, and I wanted to run with Samantha to greet them, but I kept my distance, I was wary. *She will know, seeing me. At once she will know.*

I wore shirts with sleeves that drooped past my elbows. When a shaft of light pierced my eyes, set my head throbbing again, and my neck and upper spine, I held myself rigid, I gritted my teeth and didn't cry aloud. I raided Mom's medicine cabinet for extra strength Tylenol. I stole three capsules of something prescribed for "muscle spasm pain" but decided not to take them—I might like what they did for me too much.

Daddy I can't. I can't apologize. Daddy please understand, why can't you understand.

Daddy?

***

hazy here: indistinct, vage **to soil oneself** here: to wet/dirty one's pants **doubleheader** AE double sports event **wary** cautious **to droop** to hang down **rigid** stiff **to grit** to press together **to raid** here: to search **Tylenol** American brand of medicine for relieving pain

We all watched Dad on TV. Mom, Samantha, and me. And Rabbit.

We were never nervous on Dad's account—he was so assured and spoke so well. (Unlike his cosportscasters.) The other men were intelligent and well-informed, knew players' histories, statistics, etc., but Dad knew other, more personal things. He could discuss players' individual strategies on the field, and pregame anxiety, and how it feels to be injured and expelled from the game while your teammates continue, and win. Dad interviewed a twenty-two-year-old pitcher from the Dominican Republic who spoke in halting English, and Dad was as enthusiastic and funny with him as if they'd known each other for a long time, and the interview concluded on the topic of the pitcher's youth, and Dad said, "Your generation that's inheriting the twenty-first century from us, you'll have challenges, but you have the guts and brains to deal with them. I think you young people are terrific. Good luck!" He shook hands with the young athlete, and I choked back tears—it was like Dad was shaking hands with me. I felt this was a signal to me: he knew I was watching and he'd forgiven me.

After Cape Flattery, Dad had all but ignored me. Now I felt there was a change. I could hardly breathe, I was so happy.

Mom had been wiping at her eyes during the interview, too. When it was over, she said, "Well. Your father *is* magic, isn't he?" But her voice was wistful, and I saw that she was turning the silver ring around her finger.

It was two weeks, three days after Cape Flattery when Dad returned from St. Louis. The games had gone well, TV ratings were high. Dad called happily to Samantha and me, "Girls! Tell me you missed your poor old dad." It was the first time Dad had looked me in the face since that morning at the Blounts'. I saw that yes, he'd forgiven me. I laughed and hugged him. I began to cry, I was so happy.

Dad was like that. He'd flare up in anger and say things he didn't mean; then he'd go away, and when he returned, it was as if nothing was wrong. He never said he forgave us, or he'd stopped being angry. He just laughed and forgot. And expected you to forget.

sportscaster AE sports reporter **to expel** to throw out **pitcher** AE here: baseball player **halting** (adj.) broken, imperfect **guts** (pl. inf.) courage **to choke sth. back** to suppress, hold back **TV ratings** the measured number of people viewing a TV programme **to flare up to** lose one's temper

EIGHT
skagit harbor: july 23

When Dad returned from St. Louis, there was a new atmosphere in the house. As if Dad and Mom were determined to be happy together, or to try. I heard them talking earnestly together in their bedroom at the far end of the hall. Not words but the sounds of words, a mysterious murmur.

Once, I heard what sounded like Mom sobbing— but no, it must have been Mom laughing.

I think.

The Freaky-urge came to me to eavesdrop. *Find out all you can. Knowledge is power.* But I hesitated. I was fearful of being caught.

Dad announced at breakfast that he'd be in New York City for a few days. Then he winked at Samantha and me as if he had a surprise for us, and said, "Your mother has some news for you, girls."

And Mom said, smiling, nervous and excited, "That's right. We're going to Skagit Harbor tomorrow."

I looked at Dad. For a moment I felt almost a stab of fear.

But Dad was smiling, pleased with himself. He was letting his girls go. He was making a present of Skagit Harbor to Samantha and me, and he was making a present of Samantha and me to Mom.

Why? Because he can. Because it's in his power.

Samantha squealed with excitement. (I wished she wouldn't! I knew that Dad was watching us.) Coolly, I asked, "How long will we be there, Mom?" This was a neutral question. I knew Dad would approve.

Mom blinked at me, smiling. She was turning the silver ring round and round her finger. She glanced at Dad, who appeared to be absorbed in TV news. Mom said, "How long? I—don't know, exactly." I guessed that the decision was Dad's and that Mom didn't know yet.

Skagit Harbor! I hadn't been there since, it must've been before Forrester. I was in eighth grade, maybe. And Samantha had been just a little girl.

Dad hadn't come with us then, either. Or Todd.

Funny I couldn't remember people, much. It's like you use your eyes to see but you never see yourself, so what you see, places especially, are vivid in your memory, but not you, yourself. And you see your mom and dad

to sob to weep, *schluchzen* **stab** (n) *Stich* **to squeal** to make a long high-pitched cry or sound **to approve** to accept

all the time, it's hard to remember what they used to look like. Except for photographs, a person's memory would be vague and misty.

But I remembered Skagit Harbor really well. It was an old fishing village on the Skagit River north and east of Puget Sound. West of the Cascade Mountains. An hour from Seattle, and another hour's drive and you'd be in British Columbia, Canada. Farmland, but also wilderness. Grazing cattle and horses but also miles of evergreens, blue spruce.

Mom was saying that local people in the village, especially fishermen, were having a hard time economically. But there was so much civic pride, Skagit Harbor citizens loved where they lived and were proud of their houses and gardens, even when they didn't have a lot of money. "See? It's lovely, isn't it?" Mom kept saying as she drove along Main Street to a hilly street called Harbor, and around and past First, Second, Third Streets. Samantha and I stared and stared. You could see how carefully the old Victorian houses and buildings had been preserved, even when they were a little shabby and run-down. Main Street looked prosperous, though: there were a half dozen new galleries and restaurants. Mom pointed out the Orca Gallery, a small storefront, which she said was carrying some of her new work.

At the eastern end of town, on the water, was a small harbor of rugged-looking old fishing boats and rusted barges, and at the other end of town there was a small marina of sailboats, speedboats, and yachts, which mostly belonged to summer residents, Mom said. On a hill above Harbor Street was the Skagit County Historic Museum, an old stone building like a monument to another century. There were boarded-up mills, and a fishery still in operation, and an open space that was the site of the SKAGIT HARBOR FARMERS' MARKET SAT/SUN. We drove past Hogan's Mills, where Mom said she bought just about all her household supplies. We drove past a sprawling old Victorian house painted purple whose veranda and front lawn were crowded with "antiques" and "art"—like reindeer made of crinkly silver material with strings of glitter in their antlers, and life-size human figures made of wire hangers. We drove past the Skagit Harbor Volunteer Fire Department, where men, some of them shirtless, were hosing down their fire truck, and Mom tapped her horn and the

blue spruce (bot.) *Blaufichte* **run-down** (adj.) neglected **rugged** ['rʌgid] robust **barge** (n) large flat boat **marina** harbour for yachts and small boats **boarded-up** covered with boards **sprawling** spreading out over a wide area in an unattractive way **crinkly** *zerknittert* **antler** branched horn that grows on the head of a male deer, *Geweih* **wire hanger** *Kleiderbügel aus Draht* **to hose down** to wash (a car etc.)

men waved at her. Mom said, "Everybody knows everybody else in Skagit Harbor."

Not exactly like Yarrow Heights.

At home in Yarrow Heights, nobody is ever outside where you might see them, let alone tap your horn and say hello. But in Skagit Harbor it was surprising how many people were outside, at about eleven A.M. on a weekday morning. We saw people working in gardens, trimming fruit trees (there were gnarled old apple trees in the front yards of some houses, as if this part of town had been a big orchard at one time), repairing cars and pickups in the street, playing with children. Lots of children. And dogs trotting loose. (Rabbit was quivering with excitement, leaning out a rear window and barking.) We passed a few small churches and cemeteries, a cluster of mobile homes ("Not 'trailers,' girls, remember: 'mobile homes'"), and even a big old fishing boat that looked as if it had been swept up from the river onto land in a flood, and left there, to be painted robin's-egg blue and converted into a house: the deck was a veranda crowded with furniture and children's toys and a profusion of morning glory vines. On the veranda was a pigtailed woman of about Mom's age with two small children and a Border collie, and Mom slowed the station wagon here, too, to wave and call out, "Hi there!" It was startling to hear a stranger call back, "Krista, hi!" with such fond familiarity. Mom said, driving on, "That's Melanie. She's a potter, like I'm trying to be. She's a terrific friend and neighbor."

I felt a small stab of jealousy. It was childish, I know. But I seemed to hear Mom's words as Dad might hear them, and I felt Dad's hurt. *You have no right to love strangers.*

Samantha was thrilled with the boat. She wished we could all live in a boat, on land.

Deer Point Road, which Mom jokingly called the wrong side of the tracks, was a hilly, unpaved road at the edge of Skagit Harbor. Beyond was the open countryside, dense with evergreens. Most of the houses on this road were small summer cottages and cabins painted eye-catching colors—dark gold, cobalt blue, lime green, lavender, even poppy orange.

to trim cut **gnarled** *knorrig* **orchard** area of land where fruit trees are growing **cluster of** (n) group of things of the same kind **trailer** AE caravan **robin** AE *Wanderdrossel* **profusion** mass, abundance **morning glory vines** (bot.) = Trichterwinden (Prunk~) **pigtailed** (adj.) *mit Zöpfen* **startling** surprising **potter** (n) sb. who makes clay pots by hand **lime green** pale green colour **lavender** (bot.) *Lavendel* **poppy** (bot.) *Mohnblume*

Mom's cabin, which I remembered as pretty plain and drab, had been painted maroon, with bright-yellow sunflowers like smiling faces on the shutters and along the edge of the steep-pitched roof. ("Well, I didn't do all the painting myself. I had a little help from friends and neighbors.") There was just a single front window in the cabin, a square pane of glass, and behind it was a tall clay vase Mom had made back in Yarrow Heights, filled with dried goldenrod and broom sage.

"Oh, Mom! It's so *pretty*." Samantha was sounding wistful. "Like a dollhouse."

Mom laughed. "Yes, it's about that size."

Dad had said dismissively that the cabin was no larger than our living room at home, but in fact it was smaller. I felt a twinge of claustrophobia. Not wanting to be too close to anybody, and wanting my own space. Though I hated the big old mausoleum-museum we lived in, at least it had *space*.

In Mom's narrow front yard was an ancient box elder that loomed over the cabin. Mom owned only about an acre of land, approximately half of it cultivated and the rest an open meadow filled with blooming wildflowers, Queen Anne's lace, and chicory. Mom didn't have a real driveway, only a rutted lane that came to an abrupt end at a row of staked tomato plants. She didn't have a garage, either, but an old stable she used for storage. There was another equally old, more dilapidated building, a hay barn, to the rear of the stable, which was actually on someone else's property but looked as if it might belong to Mom, and at the peak of the barn roof was a rooster weather vane.

That rooster! Suddenly I remembered. I'd been pretty young when Mom had first brought me here, and I'd made up some stories about that rooster, which was made of copper. There were roosters in the neighborhood that crowed at dawn, but to me it was the rooster on the barn roof that was crowing. Mom had pretended she'd believed me. "Yes, Francesca. He's the first to crow. He's the loudest."

drab (adj.) colourless **maroon** (adj.) of dark brownish-red colour **shutter** *Fensterladen* **steep-pitched roof** *steiles Giebeldach* **goldenrod** (bot.) *Goldrute* **broom sage** AE (bot.) wild warm season grass **wistful** regretful **dismissively** with contempt **twinge** (n) a short sudden feeling of pain **claustrophobia** [ˌklɔːstrəˈfoubjə] a strong fear of being in a small enclosed space **box elder** (bot.) *Eschenahorn* **to loom** to tower, rise **acre** about 4050 m^2 **Queen Anne's lace** (bot.) wild carrot **rutted** (adj.) marked with deep tracks made by wheels in a soft ground **to stake** to tie up **dilapidated** run-down, broken-down **rooster** AE (n) cock **weather vane** *Wetterfahne* **to crow** to make a loud high sound like that of a cock

There was my magic rooster, after so long. I'd grown up, nearly, while the rooster was still on the roof as if nothing much had changed. The barn was really old, with a sagging roof, but somebody had tried to repair it with unpainted boards. I wanted to point out my rooster to Mom and Samantha, but I felt shy suddenly.

Mom was laughing like a little girl, unlocking the cabin to let us inside. "I hope it doesn't smell stuffy. This is my studio, too." The interior of the cabin was like Mom's studio at home except cozier, with more furnishings. There was a yellow-striped sofa bed, and there were cane-backed chairs Mom had painted green, blue, and red herself, bought at the outdoor "antique shop" we'd just passed. There was a beautiful coarsely woven hemp carpet on the floor, and there were wall hangings Mom had made herself this summer, and clay pots, animal figures, and needlepoint designs. There was a skylight overhead, and a loft with a railing where Samantha and I would be sleeping together in a double bed with an old brass headboard; to get to the loft, we had to climb a ladder. I said, "Mom, this is *so cool*. I love it!"

I spoke quickly. Before I heard Dad's sneering voice in my ear. *Your mother's in her own zone now. More and more. Where you'll find her.*

NINE
skagit harbor: july 24–27

Mom said, "I feel so at peace here. The first thing I hear is roosters crowing, from that farm up the road. Sometimes I get up as early as six thirty A.M. If the mist isn't too bad, I take Rabbit out right away, down to the harbor and back. He loves it here too."

It was obvious Rabbit loved Skagit Harbor. Most of the time Mom let him run loose here, which was forbidden in Yarrow Heights. Inside Mom's little cabin, Rabbit could relax knowing that no one would scold him or allow him to know how much he was disliked.

Mom's schedule was: work in her studio through the morning, then lunch and errands in town; impromptu visits with friends; late-afternoon work in her studio, and household tasks; getting together casually in the evening with friends and neighbors. "Nothing is very formal here in

to sag to curve down, hang down **stuffy** (adj.) without fresh air **cane-backed** *mit einer Rückenlehne aus Binsen(geflecht)* **coarse** rough **hemp** (n) *Hanf* **loft** *offener Dachboden* **brass** *Messing* **sneering** (adj.) mocking, scornful **errand** (n) task **impromptu** here: spontaneous

Skagit Harbor, as you can imagine." Mom wore funky old paint-stained khaki shorts or jeans; pullover shirts; running shoes or sandals, or she went barefoot. She was long legged and had a warm golden tan, and her hair was cut short and spiky, pale red streaked with a beautiful silvery gray. She looked so happy most of the time, you'd almost have thought she was a college girl, brimming with energy and enthusiasm. She looked so free. Twyla once said *It's weird to think, isn't it, that we wouldn't be friends with most of the people in our families if we weren't related.* I'd agreed with Twyla at the time, but now I wasn't so sure.

Samantha said, "Mom, you're so much fun!"

Samantha hugged Mom, and they laughed together. I felt a stab of jealousy. Even if I felt that way, I couldn't behave like Samantha—I wasn't ten years old.

Mom told us that our aunt Vicky was planning to drive up from Portland, to visit with us on Sunday, three days away. "Vicky is eager to see all of us," Mom said. "It's been a while." I was feeling guilty about Aunt Vicky but didn't know what to say. I wondered if Mom knew how Vicky had called me, and e-mailed me, and I'd never answered. I decided no, probably Mom didn't know; Aunt Vicky would not have told her, because to tell Mom would be to indicate that she, Mom's older sister, was concerned about her. And that meant she'd been concerned about Dad. How Mom and Dad were getting along together. I imagined Mom telling Aunt Vicky, *Things are fine!* I imagined Aunt Vicky gripping Mom's shoulders in her strong hands and giving Mom a little shake and saying, *Krista, tell me the truth.*

Beyond that I couldn't imagine.

Mom must have seen a look in my face. I guess my emotions show like ripples in water, and she said, "Vicky loves Skagit Harbor too. She's going to stay for two weeks in August, in a bed-and-breakfast, if she can get away." Mom paused, smiling tentatively. "Vicky has been a little worried about us. I mean—concerned. She has the idea that things are different between your father and me, and really—they are *not*."

Samantha said, "But, Mom—"

Mom said, "No, really. Things are not changed between your father and me. We have a slightly different schedule, but that isn't so unusual. We've worked things out very well, I think."

Dad has told you to say that. Those are Dad's words.

tan (n) attractive brown colour people get after they have been in the sun **brimming with** full of **tentative** hesitant

This was a shrewd Freaky-thought. It came and went in my head, in an instant.

I said, "You and Dad seem to be getting along okay. Last week Dad was telling me, he thinks you're doing some interesting paintings."

This was not true, exactly. I said it to make Mom feel better.

Mom glanced at me, smiling but puzzled. As if she wanted to believe. "Oh yes," she said quickly, touching her throat as if to adjust a nonexistent scarf, "I—things are fine between us. They always have been."

We were outside, walking in Mom's backyard. Samantha and Rabbit ran ahead, through a meadow of wildflowers. There was a lot of loosestrife in bloom, spiky purple flowers growing on upright stems. I hoped that Mom wasn't going to ask me which paintings of hers Dad was referring to. I pointed at the weather vane rooster on the roof of the old barn and said, "I used to think he was the one who crowed, remember?" Mom glanced up at the rooster and laughed. "Francesca, you were such a—fantasist! As a little girl, you made up such stories about animals."

"I did? I don't remember."

"Well, you remember Mr Rooster. That was your name for him."

I guess I remembered. It was sort of vague. I remembered, from a long time ago, the day Daddy scolded me for "lying." For "making up things that aren't true." My grandma Connor was there, asking me about nursery school, and I must have said something fanciful and ridiculous, because Daddy interrupted, and everybody became quiet.

Mom and I tramped through the tall grass and creepers to explore the old barn from the outside. I loved the barn smell of hay and ancient dirt, grime. I loved the way swallows flew in and out of a paneless barn window, like big butterflies. Mom said that her neighbor was elderly, in her eighties, and would probably be leaving her property to children who lived in Seattle, and who wouldn't care to live in Skagit Harbor. "If I could afford it, I'd love to buy this property. There are three acres. Just think!" Mom sounded so wistful, I hardly had time to think, *But Dad makes so much money, don't we have money? Can't we afford it?*

We circled the barn and peeked through the cracks in the old weather-worn boards. Rabbit came trotting back to us and ran away through the field, with Samantha clapping and calling after him. It was a warm day, streaks of cloud overhead but a pale-blue sky. As Mom said, things were very quiet here. At one corner of the barn there was a large, sand-colored

loosestrife (bot.) *Weiderich* **creeper** (bot.) *Rankengewächs* **grime** (n) dirt, filth

boulder that must've weighed a ton, partly covered by morning glory vines, and almost hidden beneath this boulder was a burrow some creature had made. I thought it was a rabbit but Mom said no, the burrow was too big for a rabbit, probably it was a groundhog. It was an old burrow, not a new one. Maybe it wasn't even inhabited any longer. I said, "A special hiding place."

Mom said, "It is. A special hiding place. You're right, Francesca. Someone could leave a secret message for someone else in this burrow. No one would ever look here."

We hiked back to Mom's cabin, where Samantha and Rabbit had been joined by Mom's friend Melanie, her two young children, and her Border collie, Princess. The way Rabbit was making up to Princess, who was twice his size, you'd have thought he'd never seen another dog before, let alone one so beautiful.

Mom's friend Melanie was a young widow: her husband had been a trucker, hauling logs, and he'd died in a fiery crash just fifteen months before. Mom told us this after Melanie had left. I'd noticed, while Melanie was with us, drinking cranberry tea and eating oatmeal cookies Mom had baked, that neither woman alluded to a husband, deceased or living. I wondered if people in Skagit Harbor knew anything about Mom's private life. And if they knew, what they thought. To them, she was Krista Connor, which was the name Mom used to sign her art. But obviously, now that Samantha and I had showed up, Mom had a family, too.

There was a single closet in the cabin, and I saw in it only a few of Mom's clothes. Mostly shirts, jeans, slacks, what Mom called "old clothes." A long skirt, and a single pullover jersey dress, pumpkin-colored, that she wore with strands of amber beads, that I liked. A few sweaters, a lightweight canvas jacket. And only a few pairs of shoes. Back home, Mom's closet was crammed with beautiful clothes, most of them dresses. She must've owned thirty—forty?—pairs of shoes.

I didn't ask her about this. I wasn't spying on Mom. I wasn't going to tell Dad anything revealing, though I guessed he would ask me.

For the next two and a half days, Samantha and I had a wonderful time in Skagit Harbor. As if some part of us understood that it couldn't last.

boulder rock, stone **burrow** hole, tunnel **groundhog** *Murmeltier* **cranberry** (bot.) *Moosbeere* **oatmeal** *Hafermehl* **deceased** dead **closet** AE wardrobe **slacks** AE (pl.) trousers **strands of amber beads** *Bernsteinketten*

Mom took us hiking on a small mountain north of town which overlooked the harbor and, to the east, the foothills of Mount Moon, which was a much higher mountain. Melanie, her children, and Princess came with us; we packed a picnic lunch. Later, while Mom was working in her studio, an artist friend named Mero Okawa took us rowing and swimming on the Skagit River near his place, a cabin like Mom's except larger and a little showier. Everybody seemed to know everybody else in Skagit Harbor, at least in Mom's circle of Deer Point Road residents, artists, and gallery owners. I had the idea that in a week, everybody would know me. There were girls my age I met who seemed really nice, and a few guys. People began calling me Franky almost immediately, which I liked. Nobody asked me about my dad, if they knew who he was. And nobody asked where I went to school, as they would have in Seattle where the school you attend, public or private, is a shorthand way of signaling who you are, how much money your parents have.

Friday evening there was a barbecue at a neighbor's house on Mom's road, where everybody brought food and things to drink. We helped Mom make potato salad and husk sweet corn. There was a softball game before supper, and rowing on the river, by moonlight, afterward. All ages of people were together, having a great time. I have to admit, I met a boy named Garrett (a senior at Skagit Harbor High) who seemed to like me, I mean in a casual, kidding-around sort of way. He was nice to Samantha, too, and offered to take us sailing on Sunday anytime we wanted. Saturday evening, Mero Okawa invited people to his gallery first (he owned the Orca Gallery), then took about twelve guests out to dinner at this place that was everybody's favorite fresh-fish restaurant, on the river. At first I thought that Mero Okawa was sort of weird, then I really got to like him. Mom said of him he was her closest friend in Skagit Harbor, like a brother.

Mero overheard, and said, deadpan, "Krista, I hope I'm nicer than a mere brother. *My* brothers are beasts."

Mero Owaka described himself as two parts Hawaiian, one part Caucasian—"But which part is which I haven't been able to figure out." He was a "sculptor, sort of," but mostly a small-scale art entrepreneur, owner of the Orca Gallery and also a co-chair of the Skagit Harbor Arts Festival, which was scheduled for Labor Day weekend. (I heard a lot about this because other dinner guests, including Mom, were helping out too.) Mero was slender and not very tall, with stylishly bleached

to husk *schälen* **sweet corn** maize **to kid around** (inf.) to fool about **deadpan** (adj.) blank, expressionless **entrepreneur** businessman

ashy-blond hair dark at the roots, and a smooth olive skin, and eyelashes longer than most girls', including mine. He carried a Polaroid camera on a plastic strap around his neck and was always taking pictures. He wore rings on both hands, a gold chain around his neck, and a sapphire in his left earlobe. People teased Mero in a funny, affectionate way for his "fashion sense"—his "Armani look." He was really nice to Samantha and me without being condescending, like some adults. I didn't want to see this friend of Mom's as my father would, sneering at him as a "pretty boy" or, worse yet, a "fag."

That evening, Mero took Polaroid shots of Mom, Samantha, and me. He said we were "terrifically photogenic," which made us laugh. "No, seriously," Mero insisted, raising and aiming his camera, "you are. 'Krista, Francesca, Samantha: A Mother and Two Daughters.' Oh, to be John Singer Sargent, to do justice to you!" It was Mero's way to be shamelessly flattering and to make you laugh, and yet you knew that, in fact, he meant what he said.

Later, Mom said of Mero he was the "most honest" man she knew, and "probably the most good hearted."

***

Next day, Sunday, Aunt Vicky was scheduled to arrive in the early evening. She was driving up from Portland, and would be staying at a bed-and-breakfast place in town, since there wasn't room for another guest in Mom's cabin. I'd decided not to be embarrassed when I saw Aunt Vicky but just to tell her, when I had a chance, that I hadn't called her because I'd been feeling a little depressed about our family situation. But now I was feeling one hundred percent better.

Though it was Sunday, Mom didn't vary her schedule much. She dressed in her old paint-stained clothes and tied a scarf around her hair. She was preparing silk screens of big, luminescent green cattails and marsh grasses, and Samantha and I were helping her. Time really passes quickly when you're absorbed in the technical side of art! Sometime between three and four o'clock, my new friend Garrett was coming over to take Samantha and me sailing. Unless the weather suddenly turned bad: by midmorning, the sky was ribbed with darkish clouds, but there was a wind out of

condescending (adj.) patronizing **fag** (n) (sl.) *Schwuchtel, Tunte* **John Singer Sargent** (1856–1925) well-known portrait and landscape painter **silk screen** *Siebdruck* **luminescent** [ˌluːmiˈnesənt] emitting light **cattail** (bot.) *Schilf* **marsh grass** (bot.) coarse grass growing in marshes, *Spartgras*

the northwest, blowing them away. I checked the sky every few minutes, keeping my fingers crossed.

Around lunchtime, a woman friend of Mom's dropped by, and Mero Okawa bicycled over, on his way into town. The three of them were talking mostly about the arts festival. I asked Mero if it was okay if I rode his bicycle around, and he said sure. I hadn't realized how hilly Deer Point Road was—I was coasting downhill toward the harbor and enjoying myself, and would have to struggle to pedal back uphill. In between, I bicycled on First, Second, and Third Streets, which were parallel to the river and not too hilly. (I have to admit, I knew that Garrett lived on Third Street; he'd told me what his house looked like. So I pedaled past Garrett's house. It was one of the older wood-frame houses, painted a pale apple green. And there were widebranched apple trees in the front yard, and lots of flowers: I guessed Garrett's mother was a gardener. Fortunately, nobody was out in the yard or sitting on the porch, to observe me bicycling innocently past.)

When I returned to Mom's cabin, and Mero was about to take the bike from me, he asked me how did I like Skagit Harbor, and I told him I loved it. Samantha said, "I wish I could live here all the time, and go to school here. You can *walk* to school here."

Mero said, laughing, "You can walk just about anywhere here. Except on the river."

Mero had a way of fixing you with his longlashed eyes and pursing his lips, allowing you to know how intently he was listening. It was flattering, and I believed it was sincere, but it made me feel self-conscious, too. There are some people who are so naturally interested in others, and so intense about it, if you don't feel you're anything special, they make you uneasy. It's like Mero Owaka was saying to me, *Francesca, yes you're someone special. You're Freaky Green Eyes, and I know you. C'mon!*

Seeing something in my face I didn't mean to be there, Mero called me "Franky"—I'd told him to call me that, not "Francesca," as Mom did—and told me that Samantha and I had made our mother very happy these past few days. "She's been missing you girls so much. She wouldn't want me to be telling you, but—well, she loves you. She doesn't want you to be . . ." Mero's words trailed off into silence.

I felt my face burn. Doesn't want us to be— what? Hurt?

But who would hurt us?

to keep one's fingers crossed to hope that sth. will happen the way you want **porch** (n) covered entrance to a building **to purse one's lips** to press one's lips tightly as a sign of concentration **to trail off** to fade

Samantha wasn't in this exchange—she'd drifted away. But I was definitely in it. And I didn't like it. Abruptly I turned away from Mero without saying good-bye. I was afraid of crying. I felt a flash of resentment, that this man I didn't know, even if he was a nice person, and meant well, should speak so familiarly to me about things that were none of his damned business.

Mero seemed to know this too. He called after me, "Franky? Hey, I'm sorry if—"

I walked away without glancing back. Like I had somewhere to get to, fast.

It would be the last time I spoke with Mero Okawa.

This shrewd Freaky-thought.

Stay here. With Mom. For the rest of the summer.

Stay here for school, too. You could walk to Skagit High.

We were outside in the backyard helping Mom weed and trim, at about three P.M. It looked as if we'd be going sailing with Garrett—the sky was mostly a wet, washed-looking blue, storm clouds strung out at the horizon, and a good, not-too-strong wind. I kept listening for a car on Deer Point Road and glancing up every time I heard one. I tried not to feel so self conscious; I reasoned that I looked okay in jeans and a tank top, a pair of Mom's sneakers (with the kind of rubber sole, Mom said, that's good for the deck of a sailboat), and my hair in the usual ponytail except I'd shampooed it that morning, and I guess it looked pretty good. Mero Okawa had said I had "dynamite red hair" and "just the kind of freckles" to go with it, and I think he was serious, though teasing a little, too. Anyway, I was trying not to think about how I looked. I was trying to think about behaving naturally, relaxed and warm and funny. *This isn't a date—Samantha is invited, too. Keep that in mind.*

I heard a car approaching on Deer Point Road but it was going fast, and the sound of it was angry and impatient, unusual for Skagit Harbor, where the speed limit was twenty-five miles an hour in town. And when we looked up, there was a car pulling into Mom's crude little driveway and braking to a stop.

Dad climbed out of the car, leaving the door swinging open behind him. He was in shirtsleeves, but his shirt was an expensive white silk dress shirt, and he was wearing dark, perfectly creased trousers, as if he'd just

tank top sleeveless pullover **sneakers** AE gym shoes **freckles** brown spots on sb.'s skin **to go with** to match, harmonize with stepped out of an important meeting. His face was glowing with indignation and fury bright as neon. He called, "Francesca! Samantha! *Come.*"

Mom stood staring, pruning shears in her hands. It was clear she was completely surprised.

"Reid, what's wrong? I thought—"

"Girls, did you hear me? Get your things. We're leaving."

Samantha began crying and ran to Mom. I stood hesitantly, not knowing what to do. I had a big clump of yanked-out dandelions in my hands. I remembered how Dad had grabbed me at the Blounts', and it flashed through my mind that he could grab me again like that; he could grab Mom and hurt her. He was headed swiftly for us, like an athlete closing the gap between himself and his opponents. When Mom asked again what was wrong, in a faint, frightened voice, Dad seized the pruning shears from her and threw them down. He called her a name I guess I don't want to repeat.

Not that I hadn't heard that ugly word before. Sure. But never applied to my mother.

It was a confused scene. The crucial thing was, the pruning shears were on the ground and couldn't be used to hurt anybody; and Dad was relenting a little, which he often did in a situation like this, seeing we were all respectful of him, not resisting. He agreed to go inside the cabin to discuss whatever the problem was, while Samantha and I waited outside.

Samantha was crying and needed a tissue. I debated going into the cabin to get one for her but knew I'd better not. Luckily I found an old battered box of Kleenex in the back of Mom's station wagon.

Samantha whimpered, "Why is Daddy so mad? He said we could come here. He *said*."

"I guess—he changed his mind."

My heart was pounding so hard it hurt. Maybe it was an adrenaline rush. I was able to think clearly: if I heard Mom cry for help, or scream, I would run next door to Mom's neighbor and ask her to dial 911.

I would do this immediately, without hesitation. I would not go into the cabin. I would run next door.

It was like the start of a swim meet: you wait for the signal.

indignation resentment, anger **pruning shears** tool to trim the shape of a tree, bush etc. **to yank out** (inf.) to pull out **dandelions** (bot.) *Löwenzahn* **to relent** to give in, to yield **to debate sth.** to consider sth. before deciding what to do

You wait for the signal, you don't dive in before you hear the signal. You wait for the signal. That's what you do.

But there wasn't any signal. We waited for ten minutes. Then Mom appeared in the doorway with swollen, reddened eyes, a kind of sickly look, and Dad was with her, carrying Samantha's and my bags.

Mom said, "Francesca, Samantha. You're to go home with your father. Now. I've packed your things."

Samantha protested, "But, Mom—"

"Samantha, I've told you. Go with Daddy. And Francesca—"

Samantha ran to Mom and hugged her around the hips like a small, frightened child. Mom stood stiff, as if not daring to move. She repeated, "Go with Daddy, please. Samantha, Francesca. At once." Her face was masklike, rigid. Her eyes were unseeing.

I wanted to scream at her, *Why'd you bring us here if you can't keep us?*

Samantha was crying, "*You* come home, Mom! Come with us! Now!"

All Mom could do was repeat, numbly, "No. Samantha, no."

"Mommy—"

Mom pressed her hands over her ears, bent as if she'd been kicked in the stomach. She said, pleading, "No. Go away. Go away with your father. You can't stay with me, there isn't room, for God's sake *go with him*."

Dad behaved as if he wasn't hearing this. As if he was above it. Without a word he carried our bags to his car—a shining new silver Mercedes!—and placed them in the trunk. Samantha and I followed him numbly.

We didn't look back at Mom.

She was so weak, pathetic! I didn't even feel sorry for her now, I just wanted to get away from her.

Hours later, I would realize I'd forgotten about Garrett.

And much later I would realize that this was to be the last time I saw my mother.

numb without feeling, dazed **trunk** AE luggage compartment, BE boot

TEN
yarrow heights: July 27

"Your mother is in love with another man. No matter what she has told you, she has chosen him over her family. She'll have to live with her decision. We can never forgive her."

Dad's voice was trembling with indignation. But he managed to smile at us. He was holding Samantha's hand in his left hand and mine in his right hand, and he seemed almost not to know he was gripping us hard, until Samantha whimpered, just slightly. Then he released us.

"I hope you understand, girls. There's nothing to discuss, really."

Samantha wiped her nose on the edge of her hand and mumbled okay.

I guess I must've mumbled okay, too. Whatever I said, or indicated, it was the right response to Dad's words.

Because he smiled, happy now. Because he hugged us both.

"My big, beautiful girls!"

Dad introduced Samantha and me to our new housekeeper-cook, a plump, dark-skinned Peruvian woman with a shy smile. Her name was something melodic like Lorita, Loreena. She might have been thirty-five years old, or fifty-five. Dad informed us that she would be on the scene six days a week, with Sundays off. Her specialties were fried bananas, bread pudding with rice, chickpea soup, roasted chicken, grilled sea bass, and "Peruvian pizza." Dad rubbed his hands together happily. "How's that sound, girls? Pretty cool, eh?"

We beamed at Lorita, or Loreena, and she beamed at us. She was a short woman, hardly more than five feet tall. Beside her, Dad towered like a giant.

Samantha didn't ask if the new housekeeper's sixday schedule meant that Mom wasn't coming home any longer. Francesca didn't inquire, either.

In love with another man. We can never forgive her.

Did I believe these words? I don't know. Did I believe that there was a man in Mom's life? I don't know. Did I believe when I seemed to know, no, there was no man, there could be no man, Mom went away to Skagit Harbor to be free? Yet if Dad said there was a man, then there had to be a man.

And we would never forgive her.

chickpea (bot.) *Kichererbse* **sea bass** *Seebarsch*

ELEVEN
the betrayal: august 11

"Franky? Don't think this is weird or anything, okay?"

Twyla sounded embarrassed. It was rare that Twyla found herself in embarrassing situations—she was the most poised of any girl in our class at Forrester. So I was on Freaky alert. I said, trying to smile, "Twyla, sure. What?"

"Well. Your mother called me. Yesterday."

This was like somebody dropping a shoe. You just naturally waited for the second shoe to drop.

"Called you? *My* mother called *you*?"

Twyla nodded. We'd been playing tennis, and Twyla had been winning, but the games hadn't been very competitive because I wasn't in the mood to win, or to try to win: for that, you need to believe that Winning Is Worth It. My Freaky-self was thinking it's nicer to let a friend win, it's like a small gift you can give, but only if the friend doesn't know you're giving it. I was thinking how much I liked Twyla, she was like a sister to me, my own age. And I was in a frame of mind, right now, where I needed her.

Twyla said, "Your mother called, and talked with my mother a little, then asked to speak to me . . . so we talked, for a half hour or so. It was fine." Twyla paused, and this word "fine" hovered in the air between us. When you say that something is "fine," what are you saying? Twyla was sitting on a bench behind one of the tennis courts, sipping Evian water, her slim bare legs tightly crossed at the knee and locked at the ankles for extra security. Cool Twyla, trying not to squirm as I stared at her.

I hadn't spoken with my mother in more than two weeks. Since that day Dad came to get Samantha and me in Skagit Harbor. Dad was saying *Your mother is incommunicado in her own zone, girls.* I wasn't sure what that meant. If I asked Dad, I mean if I drew breath to ask, Dad shut me off with a razor-swift smile and a warning wag of his forefinger. I wondered if Mom had tried to call us and could not. I kept my cell phone turned off. I never answered the family phone and never listened to voice mail on the family line.

I never called Mom's number in Skagit Harbor. After a while, I seemed to have lost it.

betrayal disloyalty **poised** self-possessed, self-assured **alert** (n) watchfulness, caution **to hover** to float, drift **to squirm** to feel embarrassed/ashamed **incommunicado** (adj.) having no means of communication with other people, isolated **wag** (n) movement from side to side

I asked Twyla what my mother wanted.

Twyla said, "That's kind of it, Franky . . . I mean I'm not sure. It was like she just wanted to talk . . . to talk about you."

Too weird! My mother calls my best friend behind my back.

I felt a Freaky-flame pass over me. It was like my mother was betraying me. And it was none of Twyla's business what was going on in my family.

The thought came to me thrilling-scared, *Dad better not know about this betrayal.*

"Ask you about me, Twyla? Ask what?"

Twyla shrugged, frowning. Her beautiful eyes were evasive.

"Just if I'd been seeing you. Talking with you. I explained I'd been at camp, but we were getting together today, for tennis. She asked when, exactly when, like what time; and where were we playing; and if you'd been taking lessons this summer, which kind of surprised me, I mean, wouldn't your mother *know*? Gradually it dawned on me that she wasn't home. She was asking things because she hadn't talked to you in a while. I think she liked to hear me say your name—'Franky.' While she kept calling you 'Francesca.' She sounded a little different than usual, like she was sort of excited, and nervous. Finally I said, 'Mrs Pierson, is something wrong? Haven't you been seeing Franky? I thought Franky was home.' She said, 'Twyla, nothing is wrong. I'm just spending part of the summer at Skagit Harbor and it gets lonely here.'"

Twyla paused. She took a thirsty swig of water. Her perfect Twyla skin was looking less perfect, like this conversation was giving her hives.

I said, "My parents aren't separated, Twyla, if that's what you're wondering." I was trying for a Freaky-cool tone but my voice sounded like dry spaghetti cracking.

"Oh, no. I wasn't."

"This place in Skagit Harbor, it's a summer cabin Mom's family owns. She's up there for a while, doing silk screens. Pottery. A gallery there exhibits her work."

Twyla was smiling encouragingly. "Gosh, Franky. That's terrific."

"My mom and dad are not separated; it's just that my dad travels a lot for his job."

Like this was a new, astounding fact Twyla needed to be told. But she said, "Oh, I know! Reid Pierson, he's always on TV. All over."

evasive (adj.) here: eager to avoid eye-contact **swig** (n) *Schluck* **hives** (pl.) *(Nessel) Ausschlag*

"So—my mom's at this summer place. For a few weeks. Samantha and I, we were just there visiting, and we're going back again in a few days. We'll be staying till Labor Day."

Twyla asked me about Skagit Harbor, not just to be polite but also because she was genuinely interested. (I think.) An uncle of hers had a fantastic summer place in Port Greene, which wasn't far away. So I told her about Mom's cabin, and Mom's art, and how beautiful the small town was, and this guy I'd met named Garrett who was going to take me sailing soon. . . . I talked, and my voice sounded weird in my ears, earnest and eager. I wanted Twyla to know that things were fine in the Pierson family, just as they were in her family.

But I wanted to confess, *Twyla, I'm so afraid.*

I wanted to beg, *Twyla, don't tell anybody will you? Don't betray me.*

We'd had a pretty long break. It was time to resume tennis.

Heading back to the court, Twyla swung her racket to loosen up, and said, like she'd just thought of it, "Oh, Franky. When your mom hung up, she said to tell you, 'Don't forget Mr Rooster.'"

TWELVE
the call: august 25

When the phone rang at ten twenty P.M., it hit me how badly I wanted this to be Mom. I had not spoken with her since July 27: The Sunday of Betrayal. I knew that she'd been calling us. Our new housekeeper had been instructed by Dad how to deal with the absent Mrs Pierson if/when she called so that the rest of the family could be spared. I kept my cell phone turned off except when I used it, and I had not used it to call Mom and would not. Counting the days since that Sunday. *You can't stay with me, there isn't room. Go with him!*

The phone was ringing. Our housekeeper wouldn't answer it so late in the evening. Dad was still out. Todd was home for the rest of the summer but out for this evening, too. I stood paralyzed staring at the phone. My fingernails were digging into the palms of my hands. "I hate you. I don't love you. *You* go away."

I saw my hand reach out to pick up the receiver.

Labor Day annual federal holiday in the USA (on the first Monday of September)

Don't let her manipulate you, girls. She's a woman who blackmails with her emotions. The kind who betrays, and blames you for what she has done to you.

You can't live with both of us. You'll have to choose.

Samantha had chosen, like me.

Saying, "You, Daddy." A quick, frightened smile. A thumb jammed against her mouth.

And I said, swallowing hard, "Y-you, Daddy."

The words came from me hoarse and cracked. I was numb, so tired. Freaky was such a long distance from me at this moment, I could barely remember what she'd felt like.

Freaky Green Eyes? My eyes were faded green and bloodshot.

It was the right answer, though. Daddy smiled eager as a boy, and Daddy stooped to hug us. This was our reward. This was our promise. That Daddy loved us, his big beautiful girls, and he would protect us because he was strong. *Your mother has betrayed you.*

There was no need for Dad to tell us, *Your mother can't protect you.*

Mom wrote to Samantha and me, I guess. I mean, I was pretty sure. But Dad had had all our mail rerouted to a post office box. Dad had the key to this box, which was in the Yarrow Heights station. I would never see it.

The more days passed, the more disgusted I seemed to get with my mother. I kept seeing her stricken faced, bent as if she'd been kicked in the stomach, making a pushing gesture with her hands, telling Samantha to go away. *Go with him!*

We'd gone with him. We'd gone with Dad. What he was telling us of our mother: we understood how she'd betrayed us.

I didn't tell Dad about my mother calling Twyla to ask about me.

I didn't want to upset Dad more than he was.

And I was furious with Twyla, too. My so-called Best Friend. Well, maybe it's better not to have a Best Friend if she talks about you behind your back and betrays you. I could imagine Twyla on the phone telling Jenn, Marnie, Leona, *Have you heard, Mr and Mrs Pierson are separated? Mrs Pierson has moved out of the house. You can't ask Franky—she's into total, pathetic denial.* Our last three tennis games, I'd hit dynamite serves

to blackmail *erpressen* **bloodshot** (adj.) red because of broken blood-vessels in one's eyes **to stoop** to bend forward and downward **to reroute** to send sth. to a different place from the one it was originally going **stricken faced** here: depressed, deeply grieved **serve** (n) start playing in a tennis game by throwing the ball up in the air and hitting it over the net

over the net straight at Twyla, and the rest of the time I made her run panting all over the court, placing my shots with cruel precision. It was Freaky-control, mean and vengeful. My dad would've been proud of me if he'd seen! Twyla had been flattered by the tennis coach at the club into thinking she was a pretty good player for her age and size; now Freaky was exposing her. By the end of the set her face was flushed and mottled and her silky black hair was in her face. She said in this hurt, bewildered voice, "Oh, Franky! What's come over you?" At the time I felt great, but afterward when I was alone, I felt really bad.

Twyla wasn't calling me much in August. I told myself I didn't give a damn.

Now the phone was ringing, and I picked it up, and my hand trembled as I brought the receiver to my ear.

"H'lo?"

"Francesca? Thank God, you've answered."

It was her. It was Mom.

She was asking how I was and I said okay in this flat cool voice. In this voice meant to signal, *Why are you calling me, why now? I am so, so bored by this.* Mom's voice was eager and anxious. She sounded as if she had a bad cold. She sounded as if she was making every effort to speak clearly, not to stammer or break down. I shut my eyes. I could see her with Dad's eyes, in that cozy little cabin of hers where she lived her perfect, selfish life. In the dollhouse. In her own zone. She was saying how much she missed Samantha and me, how much she wanted us with her. How lonely it was there. At the same time she was begging me please not to tell my father she'd called because he had forbidden her to call, and she'd promised she wouldn't call, but she had to call, to hear my voice— "Oh, Francesca, you and Samantha know that I love you, don't you? You won't stop loving me?"

I swallowed hard. I wasn't going to break down.

I said, "You could come home, Mother. Anytime."

My mother stammered, "Francesca—no. Honey, I—c-can't."

"What do you mean you *can't*? You *can!*"

"Not any longer. Not now."

"That's a lie. Daddy says you can come back to live with us anytime you want to, except you don't want to."

"Francesca, no. Please, honey. Don't ask me to explain, this is too upsetting for the phone, I need to see you face-to-face—"

mottled covered with spots or coloured areas

I wanted to slam the receiver down. *Don't ask me to explain.*

It was like the way she'd fended Samantha off, screaming at us. *You can't stay with me, there isn't room.*

She'd begun to cry. I hated her, blackmailing me with her emotions. I knew exactly what she was doing. I was quiet for so long, she said anxiously, "Francesca, are you still there?" and I said, "Yes, Mom. Where else would I be?"

It was then I heard a car in the driveway. Possibly it was Dad coming home, which meant I'd better get off the phone. "I'm hanging up, Mother. Maybe you shouldn't call back. Samantha and I will be starting school in two weeks. If you're not back home by then, please please please don't come back ever."

"Francesca, honey—"

"I'm not 'Francesca'! I hate that name! And I hate you! Good-bye!"

The last time I spoke with Krista Connor, my mother.

THIRTEEN
the last day: august 26

When something is *the last*, you don't always realize. Like *crossing over*, it can happen without your knowing.

When I was questioned about this day, afterward, I would try to remember the chronological sequence of events. I would tell the truth. But I would not tell all the truth. For most of that day was unreal to me, like a dream broken into pieces. An ugly dream broken into ugly pieces.

All morning, I waited for the phone to ring. Suddenly I wanted to hear from Mom. I searched for Mom's number in my room—everywhere!—but couldn't find it.

I guess I knew then. I knew something was wrong.

I tried Skagit Harbor information and learned that Krista Connor's number was unlisted.

I requested Mero Okawa's number. But when I dialed it, a recording clicked on. "Hi! Mero isn't in right now but *please* leave a message. . . ."

Proudly displayed on my bulletin board were two of the Polaroids Mero had taken of Mom, Samantha, and me. I kept looking at these, as if they

to slam sth. down to bang sth. down **to fend sb. off** to defend oneself from sb.
bulletin board notice-board, *Pinnwand*

held a secret. One had been taken in the Orca Gallery in front of a gorgeous crimson silk screen of Mom's, and the other was on the windy deck of the restaurant overlooking the Skagit River. Mom stood in the middle, her arms around Samantha and me, and the three of us were smiling happily.

I saw with surprise that Mom and I were about the same height, and that our features, especially our eyes, were similar.

I was feeling numb, unreal. I didn't leave a message for Mero.

The night before, it had been my father who'd returned home while I was on the phone with Mom. I'd hung up quickly, though, and Dad hadn't suspected.

He'd knocked on the door of my room to say good night. He looked tired, with dark shadows beneath his eyes that were caked with, I guess, TV makeup he hadn't bothered to remove. Dad was on location in Seattle for some sports documentary that was being taped for the network, and he'd worked a long day, he said. And he had a sinus headache. Possibly it was some allergy kicking in. "That damned dog dander is still in this house. In the carpets. I can smell it."

I said, meaning to be helpful, "Rabbit hasn't been home in a while, though. Maybe—"

"I can smell it, I said. That damned rat terrier, it's like he was sleeping in my damned *bed*."

Next morning, Dad left for the studio at about eight A.M., but at nine thirty his assistant called to ask where Mr Pierson was. Our housekeeper answered the phone and put me on. "Francesca? This is Holly Merchant. We've been waiting for your father for forty minutes, and can't seem to get him on his cell phone. He isn't still there, is he?"

I said, "I'm sure he isn't." But I ran to Dad's bedroom to check, and looked into his study, and the family room, and the basement fitness center. Of course, Dad wasn't here. One of his cars, the new Mercedes, was gone from the garage.

Later, around noon, Holly Merchant called back to report that Dad was on location, not to worry. He'd gone first to an emergency room in Seattle to get medication for his sinus headache.

When Dad came home at about seven P.M., he was walking unsteadily, and his eyes glistened. There was something strange about him, as if he

gorgeous magnificent, wonderful **crimson** deep red **caked with** covered, encrusted with **to kick in** (inf.) to begin to have an effect **dander** here: small particles of dog (animal) skin that cause allergy **emergency room** part of a hospital that immediately helps people who are injured in an accident or extremely ill

was running a fever, and light-headed. He'd wiped the makeup partially off his face, but you could see some of it, caked and grainy, across his forehead. He repeated what Holly Merchant had said on the phone—he'd gone to an emergency room, had been put on medication with a codeine base, which had gotten him through hours of taping. He was told to eat an early dinner, take another pill, go to bed immediately afterward, and sleep for twelve hours.

So we had an early dinner, in the kitchen. The Peruvian food was tasty but sort of rich and heavy, so Dad couldn't eat much of it but tried, washing mouthfuls down with ice water and small sips of red wine. Todd was home from four weeks at a summer football camp in the Cascade Mountains, so most of the conversation was between Todd and Dad. Todd's big news was that he'd transferred from Washington State to Western Washington, in Bellingham, where he had a better chance of playing varsity football. (Evidently Dad had helped arrange for the transfer, since Todd had missed the application deadline.)

I wanted to join in the conversation—I hated it that Samantha and I were left out—so I said, smiling, "Gosh, that's great, Todd. That's great news. We'll be looking forward to football season."

Todd said, hardly glancing at me, "Sure." His attention was focused exclusively on Dad, as usual.

Todd was heavier than he'd been earlier in the summer. I guess he was getting into condition to be a linebacker. His neck and upper arms were dense with muscle. There were pimples on his forehead, and his face was ruddy, roughened. He laughed a lot but seemed jumpy. The thought came to me: *He's on steroids*.

This was a scary thought. Not just that steroids were dangerous, but Todd was the son of Reid Pierson who, like all TV sports personalities, had come out strongly against drugs for athletes.

Midway through dinner, Dad shut his eyes and murmured, "God. I'm dead." He'd eaten about half the food on his plate, and he'd drunk an entire glass of wine, which probably wasn't such a great idea with codeine medication. He tried to laugh, lurching to his feet. Samantha, Todd, and I stared at him, concerned. "C'mon, girl nurses. Your poor old dad

Western Washington university (WWU) in Bellington, a town in the north-west of Washington with about 70,000 inhabitants **varsity football** football (or other sporting events) at or of a US university or college **deadline** time limit **linebacker** in American Football a defensive player in the backfield **ruddy** reddish **jumpy** nervous, restless **steroids** *Anabolika* **scary** (adj.) frightening **to lurch to one's feet** to stand up unsteadily

needs nurses. One pretty nurse under each arm. Ooops!" It was like Dad to make a joke of being sick; he hated any kind of weakness, especially his own. So Samantha and I helped him make his way downstairs to his bedroom, while Todd followed close behind in case he needed more help. Dad was heavy, and very warm, leaning on us. It wasn't a joke—he truly needed us. By the time we got downstairs to his bedroom, we were all panting, including Todd, who was steering Dad into his room. But Dad refused to allow us to help him undress. "G'night, girls. G'night, Todd. You're terrific kids. I love you." He sat heavily on the edge of his bed, pulling at a shoe. "Hope your poor old dad makes it through the night."

Todd shut the door. The three of us stood in the hall for a long moment, waiting for Dad to call us back. But he didn't, of course. He had too much pride.

Todd turned and walked away, clearly not wanting to bother with his sisters, but we trailed after him, lonely and worried. Samantha was whimpering, "What if Daddy is sick? Bad sick?" Todd glared at us and said, "*She's* the reason he's sick. He's allergic to that woman."

"What woman? Who?"

For a confused moment I thought Todd meant our new housekeeper.

"Her. In Skagit Harbor. The whore."

"Todd!" I was so shocked, I almost couldn't speak. It was terrible to hear my brother say such a thing about our mother, and in Samantha's hearing. I protested weakly, "She's your mother, too."

Todd said, sneering, over his shoulder as he walked away, "No. She's my stepmother. She's your mother."

to trail after sb. to follow sb. in a tired way **to whimper** to make a series of low sad cries, *winseln* **whore** (n) prostitute

II
Missing

FOURTEEN
the interview: september 1

When, where did I see my mother last?

In Skagit Harbor. Sometime in July.

I guess ... I don't remember the date. I haven't thought much about it since.

Nobody can arrest me for that, can they?

No. I told you, I never heard them quarreling.

If some of my mother's things are missing from home, she must've come to get them. In the night, maybe. I don't know.

No. I never go into my mother's studio. Actually, I can't remember the last time I was in it. I never look in her closets—why should I?

No. Definitely not close.

It's my dad I'm close to. Everybody is.

I told you, I guess so. I guess I met Mero Okawa.

I remember him sort of. Unless I'm mixing him up with someone else. My mother's new friends in Skagit Harbor weren't very real to me.

Make me take a lie detector test, you don't believe me.

When did I speak to my mother last?

I'd prefer that you call her "Krista Connor." I'd prefer that you didn't constantly refer to her as my mother.

"Krista Connor" is her professional name. She signed her art with that name. In Skagit Harbor she was never "Krista Pierson." She was never our mother there. It was her decision.

She sent us away. She said the cabin was too small for us. For the three of us.

Was it too small?

I don't remember.

Ask Dad. He will tell you.

Dad will tell you the truth.

When did I speak with Krista Connor last?

How do you know it was a different time from when I saw her last?

Well, it's pretty obvious. What you're saying. You asked two separate questions. So probably you know.

• • •

Because if you know to ask two separate questions, when did I see my mother last, when did I speak with my mother last, you know that the time I spoke with Mom last must have been on the phone, not in person.

So you know that Mom called, and I picked up the phone. You would know how long the call lasted. Dad's lawyer Mr Sheehan says that you have the right to examine phone records, so you know, so why are you asking me if you know?

It was sometime in July. Late July. When she invited us to Skagit Harbor, then sent us away.

After that, I don't know. I've told you. Our housekeeper answered the phone mostly.

No. Dad has not "instructed" us to hang up if Mom calls. We make our own moral decisions, Dad says.

It was sometime in late August she called. I mean, when I answered the phone.

You know this, you have her phone records, why ask me how long we talked?

Except "we" didn't talk, really. Mom talked to me.

Why did she call?

I don't know.

I don't remember.

I've told you: I don't remember.

... Well maybe it was to say she missed us. Samantha and me.

Maybe that was it.

How long did she talk?

Before I hung up?

Why ask me, you have her phone records. Unless you're trying to trick me.

Unless this is a game.

• • •

Do I have any idea where Krista Connor is?

I told you NO I DO NOT.

NO she did not tell me where she was going. NO she did not tell me who she was going with. NO I don't know any reason why she would "disappear."

NO I am not angry with Krista Connor. I feel no emotion for Krista Connor.

None of us do. In our family.

Because she abandoned us.

Because she betrayed us.

Because she moved away from us, to live in her own zone.

She even took Rabbit with her.

Rabbit? Our Jack Russell terrier.

We miss him. It's lonely without Rabbit in our house. ... See, Mom had no right to take Rabbit away with her, that's why Dad says she's a *selfish woman*.

And now Rabbit is gone, too. "Disappeared."

NO Dad never "struck or kicked" Rabbit!

Who told you that?

NO Dad has never "struck or threatened" me. NO Dad has never "hurt" me.

And not Samantha either.

If my aunt Vicky is saying these things, she's ... lying.

If my mother's family is saying these things ...

If Mom's friends are saying these things, they are all lying, and I hate them.

Maria? Maria said ... ?

She's lying. She's confused.

No, I don't know why Maria would make up such things. Maybe Mom told her, and Mom was lying. Pretending Dad had hurt her when she'd hurt herself somehow.

Bruises on her neck. Welts. Then she'd hide them with a scarf.

No. I don't know. If she was doing these things to herself, I don't know why.

Maybe Maria wants to get back at Dad. Because he fired her he said for stealing.

Dad told us. Not her. Never her. She told us not to make her explain. She screamed at us, *Go away*! So we went away. But we don't hate her.

No, it was Dad. Driving back from Skagit Harbor. He said—

Your mother is in love with another man.

She has chosen him over her family.

We can never forgive her.

Absolutely we're on Dad's side.

• • •

No. Dad didn't say who the other man is.

No. I don't know if he knows. If she told him.

No. Dad wasn't angry. Isn't angry. *My Dad never gets angry.*

Todd is the most disgusted. Todd made Samantha and me cry saying our mother is a whore.

Do I think that Krista Connor is a ...

I don't know. I don't think about it.

I'll take a lie detector test, you don't believe me.

Yes, Todd had a different mother. Not Krista Connor. His own mother died, and Dad remarried. Todd was four, I guess. It all happened a long time ago. We never think of it.

• • •

YES Dad was home all that night. I've TOLD YOU.

YES I would know if he'd left the house. YES I would swear.

NO Dad has not told me what to say.

NO I did not discuss this with Samantha and Todd.

Mr Sheehan has said not to answer that question but that isn't the reason I'm not answering it, I'm not answering it because I've TOLD YOU I DON'T KNOW.

disgusted shocked, outraged

Yes I love him very much. He's a wonderful father, and I ... I love him very much.

Mero Okawa? I told you, I don't know anything about him.

Except I know he's "missing," too.

•••

I've told you, I don't remember. I guess he owned one of the galleries. He took Polaroid pictures of lots of people, not just us.

No. Dad never met Mero Okawa.

Yes, Dad drove to Skagit Harbor. He came to take Samantha and me home. But Dad didn't meet Mero Okawa, I know.

How do I know? I know.

Because Dad says so. Dad never lies.

I'm starting to forget lots of things. I don't sleep very well, so it's like my brain is shutting down during the day. Especially about Krista Connor, I'm starting to forget.

Because she forgot me, that's why.

Even before August 26 she was forgetting me. I can't forgive her for that.

Nobody can make me remember. It's my right to forget.

FIFTEEN
the disappearance: august 27

Here is what I know, and what I have had to imagine.

Around noon of that day, a Wednesday, when Melanie Blanchard, Krista Connor's friend and neighbor, dropped by Krista's cabin on Deer Point Road, and seeing that Krista's car was in the lane, and knowing that Krista always worked through the morning, she knocked on the door, which was a screen door, but no one answered. She saw that lights were on inside. She called through the door, "Krista? Hi, it's Melanie." No answer. Rabbit, who usually barked to greet her, did not bark. Krista did not reply. Melanie said, "Krista? Are you here?"

Melanie checked again: yes, Krista's station wagon was in the driveway. Now Melanie saw that Mero Okawa's SUV was parked at the edge of the road, in front of Krista's cabin.

Melanie pushed open the screen door and stepped inside.

She saw: an overturned cane-back chair, a clay vase of dried flowers shattered on the floor, a toppled easel, art supplies on the floor. One of Krista's handsewn quilts had been pulled off the sofa. There were stains on it . . . bloodstains? Melanie stared, horrified.

Her friend's cabin looked as if a violent wind had blown through it, knocking some things down and sparing others.

Melanie called to her collie, Princess, who'd been sniffing around out in the driveway, to come inside. Now Princess was sniffing and barking excitedly, in the cabin, at the stained quilt, turning in circles as if an invisible adversary was snapping at her.

"Krista? Are you—anywhere?"

Frightened, Melanie checked the small bathroom beside the kitchen alcove, which smelled of sweet spicy dried herbs and flowers: empty.

Melanie climbed up the ladder to check the loft: empty. The antique brass bed was neatly made up, with a quilt bedspread and several needlepoint cushions Krista had made undisturbed.

Melanie would say afterward, pressing her hand to her heart, "I knew. I knew something was wrong. Those lights burning, and things knocked down . . . and the bloodstains. Oh God, I knew."

But Melanie didn't want to be an alarmist. She checked with Krista's neighbors up and down Deer Point Road, but no one had seen Krista Connor that morning. One of them, a woman, accompanied Melanie and Princess as they walked about Krista's property, peering into the old storage shed and into the hay barn next door. On her cell phone Melanie began dialing mutual friends. First, Mero Okawa at home: a recording. At the Orca Gallery: a recording. When Melanie called other friends, they said they had not seen Krista that morning; some had seen her the previous evening, in town. She'd been at a gallery opening reception, then at dinner with a large, casual group including Mero Okawa and several other organizers of the Skagit Harbor Arts Festival. The party broke up at about ten P.M., and Krista and Mero were observed leaving together. They had more to discuss, and Mero was going to drive Krista home.

SUV Sports Utility Vehicle, kind of off-road vehicle **to topple** knock over **easel** (n) wooden frame to put a painting on while painting **quilt** (n) *Steppdecke* **adversary** (n) opponent **needlepoint cushions** *fein bestickte Kissen* **barn** large farm building for storing crops **mutual friend** a friend that two people have both

Finally, in the early afternoon, Melanie called the Skagit Harbor police. "I—I want to report a woman missing."

SIXTEEN
the vow: september 2

First he spoke in private with Todd. Then with Samantha. Then—

"Franky? You believe me, don't you?"

He was holding both my hands in his strong warm hands that were twice the size of mine. He was speaking to me earnestly and anxiously as he'd never spoken to me before.

He would protect me and never betray me as she had done.

He would not abandon me. He would fight, fight, fight to stay with me.

"Honey, I've never hurt your mother. I've never touched her. I don't know where she is, or who she's with, or why she's doing this to us. Why she would want to hurt her own family."

Dad's eyes shone with tears. Since the day that my mother, Krista Connor, was reported missing in Skagit Harbor, since police and media people were intruding into our lives, we were like a family in a fortress, surrounded by enemies. A fierce flame coursed through us, binding us together.

Dad was saying gently, "I vow to you, honey. I don't know where your mother is. She's disappeared of her own volition. It was something she'd threatened to do, many times. The police will find her, eventually. She'll be exposed. . . ."

The venetian blinds in this room, a study with heavy leather furniture and a darkened computer, were drawn. My head ached—I had to think where we were. Not at home: at Dad's lawyer's house in Pinewood Grove, a gated community on Vashon Island. Mr Sheehan had brought us here after the front-page article appeared in *The Seattle Times* with the headline—

WIFE OF REID PIERSON REPORTED
MISSING IN SKAGIT HARBOR AREA
Police Questioning Pierson, Others

vow (n) a serious promise **of one's own volition** of one's own free will **venetian blinds** (often pl.) *Jalousie* **gated community** AE area of houses surrounded by a fence or wall; its entrance is guarded

There was a large photo of my parents in glamorous evening clothes taken at a public event back in January.

After that, things happened quickly.

There had been stories on all the local TV channels. Scavengers, Mr Sheehan fumed. Strangers swarmed over our lawn and driveway—reporters, photographers, TV crews with cameras like monstrous eyes. No one could leave the house without being confronted. When Dad appeared anywhere, for instance outside police headquarters, accompanied by Mr Sheehan and one of Mr Sheehan's assistants, even more media people surrounded him. He tried to smile, as Reid Pierson always did. He tried to be gracious, but the questions were rude and abusive—"Mr Pierson? Reid? Where's your wife? What's happened to your wife? Is it true you've been separated? Is it true your wife has a lover? What have the police been asking you? What have you told them?" Hurrying Dad to a waiting limousine with dark-tinted windows so that no one could see inside, Mr Sheehan would wave these awful people angrily away, like flies.

Except, like flies, they couldn't be waved away long in public.

But now, for a while at least, we were safe. Dad had been questioned for long hours and was fully cooperating with the police investigation. Todd, Samantha, and I were staying with Dad in Mr Sheehan's big house on Vashon Island, surrounded by a ten-foot wrought-iron fence, safe. Mr Sheehan was a famous defense attorney and often brought clients to his house for protection from the media. Dad trusted him, and he told us we could trust him, too.

Now Dad was gripping my hands tight, explaining to me that what was happening was Krista Connor's way of punishing her family. Her way of revenge. "I wish I could have spared you, honey. I didn't want to tell you and Samantha this, but I have told Todd. Your mother has been trying since last spring to win you over. That's what she says—she will 'win the girls over.' Because she wants a divorce, and she wants full custody of you. She's met someone else she wants to marry. It's all about money, this thing she's staged. Blackmail. She's been demanding millions of dollars as a settlement plus monthly payments, plus child-support payments, and I've refused, because I don't want our family destroyed. I don't give a damn

scavenger (fig.) *Aasgeier* **to fume** to be furious **abusive** offensive, insulting **wrought-iron** iron formed into shapes to make fences, gates etc., *Schmiedeeisen* **custody** care, guardianship

about money. I just care about you, Samantha, and Todd. I don't believe in divorce. I refused her, and this is what she's doing, not just to me, but to all of us. . . . You believe me, honey, don't you?"

I saw in Daddy's eyes the truth shining, and the truth was love, and would protect me.

"Y-yes, Daddy."

In Daddy's strong arms I broke down and cried, really cried, for the first time since the news had come from Skagit Harbor.

SEVENTEEN
vashon island: september 3–4

"I hate her. She went *away*."

Samantha was crying all the time. Her eyes were so red veined and swollen, it was scary to see her. She wasn't eating and felt frail as a sparrow in my arms. Even her hair, which was usually so smooth and fine, was snarled up, and when I tried to comb it through, Samantha whimpered and pushed at me, as if I was hurting her on purpose.

"Samantha, come *on*. You can't let your hair get all snarls."

"Leave me alone! I hate *you*."

I wondered if Samantha was remembering how the last time we'd seen her, in the driveway beside her cabin, Mom had pushed Samantha away without thinking and cried, *Go away. There isn't room.*

In Mr Sheehan's house, which smelled of expensive liquor and cigars, Samantha and I were sharing a guest room. Our housekeeper, Lorita (that turned out to be her name), wasn't with us in Mr Sheehan's house, so it was my responsibility to care for Samantha. I didn't mind except Samantha was being very demanding, wanting to sleep with me instead of by herself. If we started out in our separate beds, within a few minutes I'd hear her whisper, "Franky? Can I come with you? I'm so scared." Most of the time I said yes. Then Samantha would get too hot, or restless, or she'd kick at the covers, or start to grind her teeth, or talk in her sleep, or wake up and start crying, and I couldn't take it—I'd sneak over into the other bed and try to sleep.

I blamed Mom. None of this would be happening, our lives so messed up, if it hadn't been for her.

Krista Connor, I mean. She wasn't "Mom" any longer.

red-veined [veind] having a pattern of red lines on a surface **frail** weak **snarled up** twisted together in an untidy mass **to sneak** to go somewhere secretly and quietly

It won't last long, Dad promised. This "siege" the Pierson family is under.

She's hiding, girls. It's her revenge. But she can't hide forever. The police will find her. This nightmare will end.

Dad wanted to postpone Samantha and me starting school next week, but I refused. It made me wild to think of missing the first days of class. Like I was sick or something! People would say, *Where's Franky? Is she ashamed to show her face?*

Actually, my friends were being wonderful. Twyla called me twice a day and left messages if I didn't feel like picking up ("Franky? Just checking in. No need to call back"); Jenn, Katy, Eleanor, Carole called or e-mailed me, and so did Meg Tyler, our swim team coach, plus other teachers from last year, and even a few guys.

I was cautious about contradicting Dad; he was in a jumpy, edgy mood all the time now, mostly talking on the phone or waiting for it to ring, but I had to tell him, "I'm starting school at Forrester with everyone else, Daddy. I've got to. Please!"

It was a Freaky-stubborn decision. I could hear the wildness in my voice. Dad and Freaky were a dangerous mixture, like gasoline and a lighted match, I had to remember the scene in the Blounts' breakfast room when Dad had grabbed me by the shoulders and shaken, shaken, shaken me when I refused to apologize. . . . "See, people will say I'm hiding out. Like I'm ashamed or something. And I'm not. I want to go back to *normal.*"

Dad was surprised by this, but impressed. "Franky, you've got guts."

"Does that mean I can start next week?"

"I'm not going to stop you, honey."

I told myself I didn't need my mother for my life. It would be weird starting school without Mom around, but last spring she'd been away half the time, and this fall she'd have been away too, in Skagit Harbor at the cabin, so there wasn't much difference in my life practically speaking, was there? If Krista Connor was "missing" or if Krista Connor was "separated" and living in some new place.

This was what I told myself in Mr Sheehan's house on Vashon Island.

siege [siːdʒ] (n) blockade **to check in** AE here: to call sb. to tell him/her that you are safe or where you are **jumpy** nervous **edgy** bad-tempered, touchy

Samantha was only in sixth grade, and lots more vulnerable than I was. I believed that I was becoming more mature under stress, while Samantha was definitely regressing. She was too restless to read for more than a few minutes lately, and she'd always loved reading. Now she was more likely to flick through the TV channels, from channel one to ninety-eight, and back again to one, staring glassy-eyed and expressionless. Samantha definitely didn't want to start school, and I agreed with Dad that she should probably stay home for a while. "At least until Mom comes back."

Dad looked at me strangely, with a faint, startled smile.

I'd made a slip, calling Krista Connor "Mom." Dad didn't like to hear that word from either of his daughters. But sometimes, in a situation like this, I didn't know what else to call her.

Mr Sheehan was all predictions and promises.

"This will be over soon. When they realize their error."

Mr Sheehan spoke in a thrilled, informed TV voice. When he and Dad were together, you'd certainly think that Michael Sheehan, not Reid Pierson, was the TV personality. (For Dad wasn't in his "up" mood much in private. Sometimes he didn't even shave. He had to conserve his energy and enthusiasm and his beaming Reid Pierson smile for when he left the house and was "on.")

Mr Sheehan said to Samantha and me, "You're brave girls! Damned brave."

Freaky figured this guy with his earnest manner for a class-A phony except he was on Dad's side. He knew the "Byzantine" ways of the criminal justice system and would guide Reid Pierson through the ordeal safely. Freaky was thinking, *Sure, for a fee. A big fee.* I knew that top defense attorneys like Michael Sheehan billed at more than three hundred dollars an hour, and even more in court.

In court?

If there was a trial.

But there can't be a trial—Mom is just hiding away. Mom is not hurt. Mom is alive. Mom is "punishing" us. Isn't she?

Mr Sheehan repeated we were "brave girls": "It's damned hard to be the daughters of a celebrity like Reid Pierson. See, the world loves celebrities,

slip (n) here: a (slight) mistake **(he) was all predictions** (he) consisted of nothing but statements about what he thought was going to happen **Byzantine** (adj.) (fig.) complicated, complex **ordeal** unpleasant experience **fee** (n) payment

especially sports heroes, but they also love to see them messed up. Cops love them, and D.A.s, because, if they can arrest them for something, anything, they get prominent coverage in all the media. Sonsabitches!" Mr Sheehan spoke so vehemently, with such support of Dad, I wanted to love him.

Except he was coaching us. He never stopped coaching us.

Already I'd been questioned by a woman from the district attorney's office. Todd had been too. (But not Samantha, who was too young, Mr Sheehan argued.) Because I was a minor, Dad and Mr Sheehan had been present. I guess I'd come off sounding kind of sullen, resentful. Mostly I'd been scared. (I have to admit.) Mr Sheehan said that I would be questioned again, and should make sure that I said what I intended to say, no more and no less. "You never give the adversary a crumb. You make them work, and give them nothing." I tried to think of the police investigation as some kind of game, a game with rules Mr Sheehan knew and would share with us, but it stayed with me that the object of the investigation was to locate Krista Connor, and that was a good, desired object. Wasn't it?

You know your mother is gone. You know she isn't coming back.

Freaky knows.

In the investigation into Krista Connor's disappearance, lots of people were being questioned. Not just our family but relatives of my mother's, friends and neighbors and acquaintances in Seattle as well as Skagit Harbor, and probably many others. (Mero Okawa's disappearance was being investigated, too, but exclusively by Skagit County police, and with far less publicity.) I was aware from TV coverage, which was intense, that woods and marshes and abandoned buildings in the Skagit County area were being searched, as well as stretches of the river and other waterways. Expert forensics detectives were working on the crime scene.

I knew that the investigation was primarily a homicide investigation, not a missing-persons investigation. But I tried not to think of it in those terms.

D.A. (District Attorney) AE (local) public official who represents the government in the prosecution of criminals **coverage** (n) reporting **sonsabitches** (sl. derog.) sons of bitches, i.e. bad or very unpleasant people **district attorney's office** AE *Staatsanwaltschaft* **resentful** displeased, aggrieved **crumb** (n) a very small piece of dry food **it stayed with me** I kept to my opinion **expert forensics detective** a doctor who examines dead people's bodies to find out how they died **homicide** murder

No! Mom isn't gone. I don't believe it.

She can't be gone. It's like Dad says, some kind of game.

We, Francesca and Samantha, must help in the game.

"Your father never left home on that night, August twenty-sixth. We've all agreed on that point, girls, yes?"

Samantha, picking at a scab on her knee, nodded yes.

Glassy-eyed Samantha, sickish pale. When Samantha wasn't crying and whining, she switched to zombie mode.

"Your father arrived home directly from the studio, we've ascertained from numerous witnesses, he was 'exhausted'—'showing the effect of the codeine medication'—when he sat down to dinner with you at about seven thirty P.M., yes? He went then to bed between eight thirty and nine P.M., he was heavily medicated to sleep for at least twelve hours. Which he did." Mr Sheehan paused for effect, smiling. He might have been addressing a vast, attentive audience. "To the extent of your knowledge, Francesca, Samantha, your father did sleep through the night, and *you would have heard him if he'd left the house, yes?* Todd has sworn to this, and you will swear to this— Francesca, Samantha?"

Samantha's head jerked in a zombie-nod. When I hesitated, Mr Sheehan stared at me, smiling harder.

"Francesca? Eh?"

I nodded too. Yes. I would swear.

"And so, girls: when you're asked, as you will be, where you believe your father was that night, if he left the house for even five minutes, you will say . . . ?"

Samantha shivered, jamming her thumb against her mouth. In a tiny voice she said, "D-Daddy was home all night. I know he was."

Mr Sheehan turned to me. His gaze was steely, shrewd. "Francesca? Be sure—they will try to trip you up if they can."

I mumbled, "I said. I told you. A hundred times."

"So one more time won't hurt, dear."

Still I hesitated. My head felt as if shattered glass was shifting about inside, and it hurt. *Freaky had been awake, Freaky had heard.*

Heard what?

Something.

But that was a dream. A dream can't be proven.

scab (n) crust that forms over a wound **zombie mode** here: the manner of a dull, apathetic person **to ascertain** to find out **to jerk** to move with a short sudden action **steely** here: cruel, ruthless **shrewd** here: calculating **to trip sb. up** to outwit sb.; cause sb. to make a mistake **proven** attested, proved

I was staring at a pattern of stains on my jogging shoe. Thinking how it happens, you buy a new pair of shoes and they're terrific-looking and yet one day, and with me it's pretty soon, they get stained and start to look just like the old shoes you've stashed away in your closet with two or three other old pairs you haven't gotten around to tossing away yet. Thinking how fast it can happen, and the shoes are definitely not-new any longer.

A car in the driveway, headlights turned off. A door at the far end of the hall opening. Footsteps?

Definitely can't be proven.

The glowing-green numerals on the digital clock floating in the darkness beside the bed. Freaky's wide-awake eyes seeing 4:38 A.M.

Can't! Can't be proven.

When Mr Sheehan sweated, his cologne scent turned just slightly rancid, as it was now. He was staring at me, and smiling hard. Samantha, who'd been too listless to glance at me for most of the day, now stared at me too, her thumb jammed against her mouth. I wondered for a nervous moment if I'd uttered some sound, if I'd whimpered or whispered to myself.

"Yes. Sure. I've told you. I can swear: Daddy was home all that night, Daddy never left the house for five minutes, I would've heard Daddy if he had. I swear."

EIGHTEEN
freaky-logic: september 4

Freaky reasoned it out. It was simple as figuring the sides of an equilateral triangle are all equal. *If Mom is gone and isn't coming back ever, there is Dad. There is Daddy who loves you. There is only Daddy who loves you.*

to stash away to store **to toss away** to throw away **cologne scent** smell of "Eau-de-Cologne" **rancid** sour **listless** lethargic, lifeless **to reason sth. out** to find an answer/solution to sth. **to figure** to calculate **equilateral triangle** a geometrical flat shape whose three sides are all the same length

NINETEEN
freaky green eyes: first day of school, september 8

There she is. . . .

Which one? The redhead?

That's Franky.

Franky who?

Don't stare for God's sake! You know, Franky Pierson. Reid Pierson's daughter.

Oh my God. Her?

Her.

How's Franky taking it?

It's weird. But you know Franky, pretending nothing is wrong.

***

I think it's shitty. Franky's dad didn't do it. I'd never believe anything like that about Reid Pierson.

I wouldn't either! Reid Pierson is terrific.

He is so, so handsome. And sweet. My mom has a crush on him.

My mom too!

So, if he didn't do it, who did?

Do what? Nobody's found any body. Yet.

My homeroom assignment was a good one, with a teacher everybody liked, and three of my friends including Twyla were assigned to her room, too. And my classes looked promising, at least biology and art and junior honors English, which was a seminar with only seven students taught by a teacher who was also a poet. And Twyla asked if I'd like to have lunch just with her and Jenn, or with a larger table (as we usually did in the cafeteria), and I thanked her and said I wasn't hungry and was going to the library instead. (Which was true, though I ate in about five minutes out of vending machines in the common room.) Everybody was nice, mostly. At least to my face.

shitty (adj.) very bad, unpleasant **to have a crush on sb.** to have a strong feeling of romantic love for sb. **homeroom assignment** here: *Zuteilung, Zuweisung der neuen Klasse* **junior** AE relating to the final year of High School **vending machine** machine operated by money for the sale of small items (drinks, ice-cream, sandwiches etc.)

Except: our headmaster, Mr Whitney, who'd been trying to get my father to visit Forrester for years ("Just to say hello, and perhaps share a glass of sherry in my office") was definitely avoiding me. Where always he'd call out, "Francesca! Hello," now when I happened to pass him in the hall, where he was standing talking with several seniors, he saw me, seemed to freeze for an instant, then turned away just slightly, but unmistakably, as if he'd seen something deformed. In my Freaky-somber voice, I called out, "H'lo, Mr Whitney," just to let the hypocrite know I was aware of him.

Suddenly after that it seemed pretty obvious that everybody was watching me, out of the corners of their eyes. Peeking around the edges of their lockers. On the stairs, glancing back over their shoulders. In my afternoon classes my teachers seemed embarrassed at reading my name off the roll—"Francesca Pierson?"—and when I raised my hand and said, "Here," there was silence in the room, and I knew that everybody behind me was staring at me, and everybody in front of me was deliberately not turning to look.

My teachers knew who I was, of course. A new student in their classes but they knew. I saw their eyes swimming in sympathy like I was a leper they could pity but not get too close to, for maybe my condition was contagious. *Poor girl! Her mother is missing. Her father is being quetioned by police. And you know who the father is, don't you?* Almost, I could hear these words like gnats buzzing in my ears. I was maintaining Freaky-control, however, till the middle of fifth-period social studies, when somthing hit me like a wave, a cold, sick sensation in my stomach, and I knew I couldn't make it through the rest of the class. In a feeble gesture I raised my hand to signal the teacher that I was feeling desperately lousy, and with my head down and eyes lowered and my backpack gripped against my chest, I half ran out of the room.

In the rest room I was sick with a sudden attack of diarrhea. It was like my guts were on fire. I was shivering, too. I was so weak, I had to stagger down to the infirmary, where the nurse took one look at my face, made me lie down, took my temperature (it was 100°F, what the nurse called a mild fever), gave me two Advils, and told me I might be coming down with flu.

somber gloomy, cheerless **hypocrite** (n) pretender, phoney **leper** (n) sb. who has a very serious infectious disease (leprosy) **contagious** infectious **gnat** (n) *Mücke* **to buzz** to make a continuous sound like that of a bee **lousy** awful, miserable **diarrhea** AE (BE diarrhoea) *Durchfall* **guts** (inf.) the stomach and the internal organs around it **100°F** i.e. 37.8°C **Advil** trade name for "ibuprofen" effective against minor pain like aspirin

I lay shivering beneath a cover wondering: did the nurse know me? Did she know whose daughter I was? Would she be telling everyone she met afterward in a thrilled voice, *Guess who was in the infirmary this afternoon with the flu?*

TWENTY
aunt vicky and the giant atlas moth: september 9

I'd steeled myself with Freaky-resolve not to give in, but as soon as my aunt Vicky saw me, and rushed to hug me, I couldn't help hugging her back. She caught me in her arms like I'd been falling, and she was saving me, and I felt her trembling against me, and it was so completely weird, the thought came to me, *This isn't Aunt Vicky, it's somebody else.* Because she was so changed, even her voice.

"We have to hope, Franky. We have to pray. She might be—*must* be—all right."

Aunt Vicky was my mother's older sister by three or four years. A tall woman, usually strong looking, in excellent condition from hiking, backpacking, running. In her family, Aunt Vicky was criticized—and admired—for never having married, for being independent—"doing her own thing." Now she was nervous, emotional. It was a shock to see her looking so drawn and haggard. Her hair, which was a faded red, grayer than my mother's, was brushed back flat from her face so that she looked exposed, sort of blunt and raw, weatherworn. Dad hadn't wanted me to see Aunt Vicky—they'd never gotten along very well— but he'd seemed to admire her, to a degree, in the past. Dad used to say that Krista was the beautiful Connor sister and Vicky was the one with the brains. He'd meant this to be praise, I guess, but it came off sounding like both Krista and Vicky were missing something crucial.

Now Aunt Vicky's eyes were raw and reddened like Samantha's, and her voice was shaky. I hated to see her like this!

She was saying, almost begging, "Franky, are you all right? How are you and Samantha?"

I shrugged. I hated being asked this question every time an adult saw me.

thrilled excited **giant atlas moth** with a wing span of about 6 inches it is the biggest moth in the world **drawn** (adj.) exhausted, worn-out **haggard** here: worried, troubled **exposed** (adj.) unprotected **blunt** (adj.) dull **raw** (adj.) coarse, having a rough surface **weatherworn** (adj.) here: looking sad, worried and tired

And I wasn't going to tell the truth anyway, like I'd been having the most disgusting repulsive stomach trouble and my period had come eleven days early this month and the cramps just about knocked me out and I couldn't sleep for more than an hour at a time and my dreams were psychotic and I was confused, angry. Like hell I was going to tell anyone, even Aunt Vicky who I knew loved me, what was in my heart.

My mother ran away. She left us.

Why should we care about her, now?

Aunt Vicky held my shoulders, and gazed searchingly into my eyes. "Tell me anything you know about your mother, Franky, please? The last time you were with her? That Sunday, when I came up? And you and Samantha were gone? And—oh, anything! Tell me anything."

It's awful when an adult begs you. And you feel so bad you can't give them what they want, and you hate them for doing this to you.

Dad had warned me that my aunt would ask "prying"—"hostile"—questions. Like the police. Dad had warned me that I should be very careful what I told Aunt Vicky, because she was "on your mother's side"—"our enemy." Dad believed that my aunt had never approved of her younger sister's marriage to him, and that everything she said of Reid Pierson was tainted with her prejudice. She hated sports, Dad said, so she hated him.

Aunt Vicky was asking me about that Sunday. When Dad drove to Skagit Harbor to take Samantha and me home. If, while he and Mom were together in the cabin, I'd happened to overhear—anything?

Quickly I shook my head no.

But Aunt Vicky didn't believe me. "Franky, look at me. Look me in the eye. I know what you've been telling the police, but—please, will you tell me?"

I shut my eyes, shook my head. I felt my ponytail slap against my back.

Aunt Vicky said, suddenly emotional, "Oh, Franky, I'm afraid—your father has been—has—" She broke off, her eyes brimming with tears. Whatever it was, Aunt Vicky couldn't bring herself to say it.

Striking her. Abusing her. Threatening her.

I backed off, suddenly emotional myself. A panicked rage came over me like flame. "Aunt Vicky, I don't know where Mom is."

"Franky, wait—"

"Leave me alone!"

repulsive extremely unpleasant **like hell** not at all **prying** (adj.) inquisitive, impertinently curious **tainted with** here: affected with, subject to **to back off** here: to become agitated and troubled

I ran out of the room. Pressed my hands hard over my ears so I couldn't hear Aunt Vicky calling after me.

In eighth grade, when I made the swim team at school, Dad was so proud of me, he allowed me to go with Aunt Vicky on one of her trips to the Southwest. Just five days, but we had a spectacular time hiking and sight-seeing. One of the places I remember was a tropical garden attached to a natural history museum in Albuquerque, New Mexico. I loved it: giant trees and vines, gorgeous jungle flowers; so many butterflies, some as large as my outstretched hand, brightly colored as if they'd been painted, behaving like they were tame. And chattering birds everywhere. It was a rain-forest atmosphere, the air so humid you could feel moisture congealing on your skin. My favorite birds were the big white cockatoos and the Amazon parrots, with their beautiful bright-green feathers trimmed in crimson and their amazing, aware eyes. There was Daisy, who squawked, "H'lo! Pretty girl! Pret-ty girl!" when Aunt Vicky and I peered at her, and I was going to pet her head except Aunt Vicky caught my hand in time. On Daisy's perch was a comical little warning: *I bite. I hate myself afterward but I bite. Be warned!*

The weirdest things in the garden were the giant Atlas moths.

They were big, beautiful moths you'd have thought were butterflies, almost the size of bats, clustered on tree trunks and vines. Some of them you could hardly see, they blended so with the trees. They were the color of brownish mist, with dappled spots on their wings. Aunt Vicky said she'd timed our visit because this was their mating season, which occurred only every five years. And you could see the moths mating, sort of: one big dappled moth lying on another, slightly smaller moth, unmoving. At least they were unmoving while we looked.

What's remarkable about this moth species, Aunt Vicky said, is that the moths spend five years in their cocoons and only three to five days "alive" as moths. They're born with reproductive systems but not digestive systems! Once out of their cocoons, they have only a few days to mate before they shrivel up and die. "But a new generation emerges to continue the cycle." Aunt Vicky spoke as if this was good news.

moisture wetness **to congeal** here: to harden **cockatoo** *Kakadu* **trimmed in** decorated with **to squawk** to scream, shriek **perch** (n) stick or branch where a bird rests **to cluster** to gather, crowd **to blend with sth.** to match sth. or be similar to it so that you can hardly notice it **dappled** *scheckig* **mating season** period when animals have sex to produce babies **to mate** to couple, copulate **reproductive** *Fortpflanzungs~* **to shrivel up** to dry up, wither

I laughed and shuddered. "I'm glad I'm not a giant Atlas moth."

"Yes, Franky, but to the moths, three to five days *is* their lifetime. It probably feels just long enough."

"Oh, Aunt Vicky! That's just like you."

"Nature has mysterious ways, Franky. But somehow it all makes sense."

I knew Aunt Vicky had been trained as a biologist and ecologist. Still, I was stubborn and had to say, "Maybe nature doesn't make sense at all, Aunt Vicky. Maybe people like you want to think it does."

Three years later, I thought of that conversation. Aunt Vicky insisting that things make sense and turn out basically all right, the way she was saying that, thirteen days after Krista Connor and Mero Okawa were reported missing, things might turn out all right for them, too.

TWENTY-ONE
the investigation: august 27–september 9

"I miss Rabbit. *I want Rabbit back.*"

Samantha spoke sadly but listlessly. Knowing it meant nothing, what she wanted.

After so many days of searching in Skagit County by police, rescue workers, volunteers, Krista Connor and Mero Okawa were still missing. And so was Krista Connor's dog, Rabbit.

In the news items, the missing dog was rarely mentioned. Nobody cared about Rabbit. Except Samantha and me. I wanted Rabbit to be alive, so badly. Sometimes I'd shut my eyes so I could hear better his toenails clicking on the floorboards, and his breathless little high-pitched bark. *Hey! Hi! Here I am!*

I didn't tell Samantha something I'd learned from clicking onto one of the case's websites: that the bloodstains found on Krista Connor's quilt had been identified as "nonhuman."

It hadn't been Krista Connor's blood, or Mero Okawa's blood; it had been Rabbit's blood. I knew.

He'd been barking, trying to bite, protecting his mistress. A brave, feisty little dog any sizable boy or man could kill by kicking hard, and repeatedly.

feisty ['faisti] (inf.) quarrelsome, aggressive **sizable** rather big

We never discussed the police investigation in our family.

By "our family" I mean our reduced family: Dad, Todd, Samantha, me.

We never spoke of Krista Connor directly. Mostly, *she was she, her*. A missing person like a missing object. Mero Okawa was rarely alluded to— it was easy to forget Mero Okawa, but when he was spoken of, the name was simply "Okawa."

Only Dad and Mr Sheehan uttered that name— "Okawa." With a look of disdain, disgust. As if they had a bad taste in their mouths.

If you read the papers or watched TV, it seemed clear that the missing individuals had been a "couple." Because they were missing together, and Mero Okawa's SUV had been parked at Krista Connor's cabin through the night, it was assumed that they were lovers, or somehow involved. Friends and neighbors in Skagit Harbor vehemently denied this, but no one took them seriously. There was a collective wish to believe that the missing woman, separated from her celebrity husband, had been having an affair with a local art gallery owner, and that their affair, an adulterous affair on the woman's part, was the probable reason for their disappearance. The general belief was that the celebrity husband had had something to do with this disappearance, but a counterbelief was that the couple had run off together. In the *Seattle Star*, a tabloid paper, an unidentified "intimate" of Mero Okawa testified that Okawa was a "quick-tempered man with a history of domestic violence." On *Seattle After Hours*, a late-night talk show on cable, the possibility of Krista Connor having been "abducted" by Mero Okawa was earnestly discussed.

The missing couple had been sighted in Las Vegas, in Palm Springs, in Kailua Bay, Hawaii.

Mr Sheehan conceded to the press that his client and Krista Connor had been discussing an "amicable separation" but not divorce.

Neither Reid Pierson nor his wife, Krista Connor, believed in divorce, Mr Sheehan insisted. There may have been another man in the picture ("about whom my client knows nothing"), but in fact the Piersons had been on the verge of reconciling when Krista Connor disappeared.

When I read this, on the website, I felt a stab of hope. Mom is coming home? Is this so?

Wanting so Freaky-bad to believe.

disdain (n) contempt **adulterous** unfaithful, *ehebrecherisch* **tabloid paper** newspaper that has small pages containing light or popular news stories and many photographs **intimate** (n) close friend **to abduct** to kidnap **to concede** to admit **amicable** (adj.) ['æ-mikəbl] based on polite discussion and without quarreling, friendly

"What did your aunt Vicky want, Franky?"

Dad's voice was friendly, easy. But I saw the tension in his jaw. He wasn't doing TV lately—he was still on the network payroll, but his sportscasting duties had been "temporarily suspended" (according to *The Seattle Times*), so he was restless and kept a sharp eye on his daughters. I said, "Oh, just to talk, Daddy. Nothing."

"Sowing seeds of discontent, eh? Like all that family."

I bit my lip. Didn't know what to say. My Freaky-sullen heart beat hard.

"I suppose Aunt Vicky was asking about me, eh? Casting suspicion on me. Like I'm not sick with this, crushed with grief, as much as she is, in fact more. I'm the husband, for Christ's sake!" Dad was wiping angrily at his eyes. He had a sinus headache all the time now, he said. Medication didn't help. "Did you tell her that? The nosy Big Sister?"

I said uneasily, "Aunt Vicky's okay, Daddy. She's worried about . . . her sister."

"Well, she should be. Disappearing like that. With her 'native' lover. They're saying this *Okawa* is a nutcase, too. Involved with young boys. Sadomasochistic sick stuff. Like on the Internet. Your deluded mother was taken in." Dad shook his head sadly.

I had never heard this before! A Freaky-defiant urge rose in me to resist.

"The Connors are a dysfunctional family par excellence. They're suspicious, paranoid. They've 'broken off all relations' with me, their lawyer has informed the public. Nice, eh?"

I wasn't sure what Dad meant, but knew better than to ask.

"Next time your aunt Vicky comes to this house, I want to be present. I want Mike Sheehan present. I don't want that sick, man-hating female poisoning my daughter's mind, the way she poisoned her sister's mind. All the Connors have been bearing false witness about me to the police. I'll never forgive them. And neither will you."

Daddy was looking so sick, so sad, I wanted to hug him. But I was afraid to touch him.

"Okay, Daddy."

payroll list of people employed by a company **discontent** (n) here: disharmony, resentment **sullen** (adj.) ill-humoured **nosy** eager to find out other people's private affairs, prying **nutcase** (inf.) madman, idiot **to delude** to mislead, deceive **defiant** here: rebellious, obstinate **dysfunctional** (adj.) with an abnormality of social behaviour **to bear false witness** (fml.) to make wrong statements

"Todd's on my side. Todd's my boy from way back. Todd knows the score. *She* broke that boy's heart, pretending to be a true mother to him when she wasn't even fit to be a stepmother. And you, sweetie, and Sam-Sam. You're all on your daddy's side, eh? When she shows up alive and well, the police are going to arrest her. And know what I'm going to do? Sue her! For dragging her family through this dirt, for trying to destroy us. Trying to ruin Reid Pierson's career. And you kids will testify on my behalf, won't you."

It wasn't a question, it was a command.

"Franky? My big girl? You're on your daddy's team, eh?"

"Yes, Daddy."

"It could get nasty. Nastier. When *she* comes back."

Dad spoke with such conviction, grimacing as you'd never see him on TV, I believed he must speak the truth.

When she comes back.

TWENTY-TWO
the don spence show: september 10

The voice was impassioned, sincere.

"Know what I think, I think it's like the thrill in a crowd when a man, a star athlete, is injured and carried off the field. They love you, but boy! they sure want to bring you down, down, down to their own level."

It wasn't Reid Pierson saying these impassioned words but his interviewer, moppy-haired Don Spence of the local, popular *Don Spence Show*.

"Well, Don, I guess . . . I wouldn't disagree with you exactly," Dad was saying, with a faint, frowning smile, like a man who's trying to be meticulous in his judgments, "but I think it's an entirely unconscious thing, you know? It isn't conscious."

"It isn't conscious. But it's real."

"Oh, wow. Man, I can testify to that: It's real." Dad laughed, shaking his head gravely.

Don Spence was interviewing Reid Pierson, a friendly colleague-rival of many years. Sometimes he was unpredictable, even cruel to the hapless

score here: reason, cause **to sue sb.** to take legal action against sb. **nasty** unpleasant **thrill** excitement **moppy** thick, resembling a mop **meticulous** (adj.) (ultra-) careful **wow** (interj. inf.) great, excellent **hapless** unfortunate, luckless

guests on his show; but generally he was warm, friendly, funny, fair-minded. They were rivals, on competing networks, but, well—"There's no better sportscaster on the air right now than Reid Pierson," Don Spence said, after he'd welcomed his guest on the show and shaken his hand vigorously. "I'm not saying this to flatter, y'know Don Spence does not flatter. I'm saying it because it's true."

"Don, thanks. I appreciate that."

Daddy spoke humbly, for a moment looking as if he was blinking away tears.

How handsome Daddy was! He looked almost like a young man. His posture was perfect, his head held high. The bruiselike rings around his eyes seemed to have vanished. The pinched, pained expression in his face we'd been seeing for weeks seemed to have vanished. His manner was somber, for he was on *The Don Spence Show* to discuss his wife's disappearance under very suspicious circumstances, but he was able to smile, too, at appropriate times.

Todd, Samantha, and I were watching the interview in our house in Yarrow Heights. (We'd moved back, now that the media vultures, as Dad called them, were less intrusive.) Todd was taping the program, as he'd been taping news programs and local talk shows since August 27, with the intention of establishing an "archive" for Dad. His fall term at Western Washington didn't begin for another two weeks. By then, Todd believed, the missing persons case would be solved. By then, we could get on with our normal lives.

I believed this, too. I'd gone back to school after my first, difficult day and intended to keep going. It was Freaky-logic to think *One day, one hour at a time. You can do it!*

Don Spence was firing questions at Reid Pierson in his frank, candid way, and Reid Pierson was answering in a frank, candid voice:

"Do you know the whereabouts of your wife, Reid?"

"No, Don. I do not."

"Did you have anything to do with her disappearance, Reid?"

"No, Don. Absolutely not."

"You aren't in contact with her, are you?"

"I wish I was. But no."

"Are you acquainted with Mero Okawa?"

vigorously strongly **posture** (n) here: the way you position your body when sitting **pinched** (adj.) stressed, strained **pained** upset **vulture** *Geier* **intrusive** affecting sb.'s private life in an unwanted and annoying way **fall** AE autumn **candid** (adj.) here: straightforward

"I am not."

"Never met the man?"

"Never laid eyes on him."

"Is there any truth, Reid, to rumors that your wife, Krista, has been seeking a divorce?"

"Absolutely not, Don. Absolutely *not*."

Dad became almost emotional answering this last question.

After an advertising break *The Don Spence Show* returned with a pre-taped segment. This took us by surprise: close-up video shots of our parents! Dad and Mom were younger, happily smiling, very attractive. I felt a choking sensation in my throat. I wasn't prepared for this. There were photos of Mr and Mrs Reid Pierson with their family: tall, good-looking Todd ("twenty-year-old son of Reid Pierson from his first marriage") and the Piersons' daughters ("Francesca, now fifteen, and Samantha, ten").

Samantha, on the sofa beside me, made a faint whimpering noise like a frightened kitten. "Oh. Mom*my*."

I blinked away tears. I decided to be mortified, embarrassed by seeing myself on TV. Magnified on the giant screen on the wall of our family room.

Samantha was whimpering, "I want Mommy back. Why doesn't Mommy come *back*, Daddy said she's *hiding*."

Todd said sharply, "Shut up, Samantha. I'm trying to hear this."

Next were "highlights of the popular football player's career." Then brief interviews with well-known personalities who wanted to vouch for Reid Pierson: the Seahawks' manager, sportswriters, former Seattle mayor Brock Hawley, who'd been Dad's friend for years, the Seattle businessman-philanthropist Bud Blount. Mr Blount was saying earnestly, "What's happening here, this trial by media, makes me damned angry. 'Innocent till proven guilty' is the American way of life. Anyone who knows Reid Pierson will vouch for him as a good, loving husband and father, and a straight-up, decent guy. What I think, frankly, I think this is some marital spat, a lovers' quarrel, something personal and private that got out of hand. . . ."

Next there came onto the screen video clips and photos of Reid Pierson in his mid twenties, with a very blond and very beautiful young woman—

to pretape record on tape before a live show **to choke** to suffocate, *ersticken* **kitten** a young cat **mortified** (adj.) here: displeased **to magnify** to enlarge **to vouch for sb./sth.** *sich für jmdn./etw. verbürgen* **marital spat** (inf.) short unimportant quarrel between husband and wife **out of hand** out of control

"Bonnie Lynn Byers of Los Angeles, Reid Pierson's first wife." There were stills of Bonnie Lynn Byers as a fashion model and video clips of the young couple dancing at their wedding; there were photos of the Piersons at the 1983 Governor's New Year's Eve ball, and in dazzling white sports clothes on the deck of a friend's yacht in 1984. Don Spence's voice-over continued with dramatic urgency, imposed upon shots of gliding sailboats: "The first Mrs Pierson died abruptly in June 1985 in what were considered mysterious circumstances—a sailing accident on Puget Sound to which Reid Pierson was the sole witness." A collage of more photos, close-ups of Reid Pierson looking distraught, shielding his face from photographers, as Don Spence's voice continued, "The county medical examiner ruled accidental death, but there was pressure on the Seattle district attorney to conduct a more thorough investigation; eventually the controversial case was resolved with a confirmation of the original verdict of accidental death. Within two years, Reid Pierson was to remarry."

As soon as Bonnie Lynn Byers came onto the TV screen, Todd reacted as if in pain. He murmured what sounded like "Oh, God." A can of beer he'd been holding in his right hand fell from his fingers onto the carpet unnoticed by him. Samantha and I looked fearfully at our big brother, hoping he wouldn't lash out at us, but his expression was blank, rigid. His eyes were glassy, narrowed almost shut.

As *The Don Spence Show* broke for another, jangling sequence of noisy ads, Todd heaved himself to his feet and staggered out of the room.

Samantha whispered, "She was Todd's mommy? She's pretty."

I knew I should run after Todd. Seeing his mother on TV like that, with no warning, was a shock to me—I could barely imagine what it must be to Todd. But Freaky knew better. *Leave him alone. He doesn't want you.*

Frankly, I was afraid of my brother. Since Mom's disappearance, and that time he'd called her a "whore," Todd's personality was definitely volatile— unpredictable. At Mr Sheehan's house and now back home, Todd spent hours working out on fitness machines and lifting weights. He boasted he could bench press his own weight, two hundred twelve pounds.

The Don Spence Show resumed, now with Don Spence and his guest Reid Pierson live in the studio as before. You could see that the two men

still(s) (n) photo(s) of a scene from a film **dazzling** (adj.) extremely bright **voice-over** (n) voice of an unseen commentator heard during a film or TV programme **to impose upon** here: to comment on **distraught** (adj.) worried, upset **to rule** here: to make a judgement, decree **to lash out at sb.** to hit out at, strike sb. **to jangle** to speak in a noisy, babbling and intense manner **volatile** changeable **to resume** to restart

had been talking together, even laughing, during the taped segment; obviously, Dad had no idea of what had been broadcast and seen by hundreds of thousands of viewers. And Don Spence didn't give the slightest sign, how he'd stabbed his "friend and rival" in the back. He concluded the interview with an enthusiastic remark to the effect that Bud Blount was certainly right, it's the American way of justice, "innocent till proven guilty." Dad was allowed the final words, peering into the TV camera: "I just want to appeal to everyone—anyone!—who might have vital information about my wife, Krista Pierson, who's been missing since August twenty-seventh. Please help us! We are offering a fifty-thousand-dollar reward to anyone who provides information leading to Krista's return. And, Krista"—here Dad's voice began to quaver, and tears flooded his eyes—"if you're watching this, please, darling please, let me hear from you. Please come back. I love you, darling, we all love you and miss you. Krista, *please*."

Samantha was bawling now, so I had to hold her. Staring at the TV screen as the camera drew back to show Don Spence and Reid Pierson seated companionably together, talking out of earshot, as the theme music came up, loud.

TWENTY-THREE
remember mr rooster!

. . . I was bicycling somewhere almost familiar, I was in a hurry and anxious and my heart was beating fast. Where was this place? Hilly, with a smell of water? I couldn't see very clearly. There were houses, I guess, but wide spaces between them, and their colors were vague. *Mom? Mommy?* I was trying to be Freaky Green Eyes, but I was afraid, and Freaky is never afraid. I seemed to know that if I got where I was headed, I would be safe, but there was a problem with the bicycle, it was Mero Okawa's bicycle and the handlebars were too high and the wheels were weirdly asymmetrical, I couldn't keep my balance and kept falling. *Mom? Where are you?* My voice wasn't my own but a much younger voice.

There was a pale-green house floating by the side of the road, with big, spreading apple trees in the front yard. I knew that this was an important house but I couldn't remember why. Suddenly I saw the river—it was

to stab sb. in the back to betray sb. **vital** of the utmost importance **to quaver** to tremble **to bawl** to cry loudly

meant to be the Skagit River, I knew. I was trying to pedal on Deer Point Road, to Mom's cabin, but the road was uphill and no matter how hard I tried, I couldn't make the pedals turn though I was Freaky Green Eyes, and knew what I wanted, and wasn't afraid.

Mommy! Help me.

A rooster began to crow. I recognized him: Mr Rooster! He was perched on the peak of the old hay barn. I wiped at my eyes and could almost see him. He was confused somehow with a parrot with brightgreen feathers but actually he was Mr Rooster, and he knew me. That was why he was crowing: to encourage me.

But the crowing was in the room with me, and waking me. I opened my eyes, confused.

It was Samantha crying, in her sleep. She'd crept into my room and was lying curled up like a kitten on the outside of the covers, near the foot of the bed. As if she'd been fearful of crawling under the covers with me and waking me.

TWENTY-FOUR
the secret burrow: september 11

Next morning I took the nine-thirty-five Greyhound bus from Seattle to Skagit Harbor.

I guess I behaved what you'd call recklessly. I made my decision fast. It was Freaky-impulsive but I knew it was right, after that dream of Mr Rooster calling me.

Without a car, it's so hard to get around. I ended up taking a city bus from Yarrow Heights to downtown Seattle, across the floating bridge; I wasn't even sure where the Greyhound terminal was—I'd never been there before. I've taken lots of ferries, but not many buses. This bus seemed to take forever! I was anxious, I guess I was a little paranoid, thinking somebody might recognize me from that fleeting glimpse of "Francesca Pierson" on *The Don Spence Show* the night before.

Then, at the Greyhound station, which was crowded with the kinds of characters you don't see at airports, I became worried somebody might not only recognize me, but recognize me and call my father, or the Seattle police. *Where are you going, miss? Why aren't you in school?* I hid in the

Greyhound biggest North American intercity bus company **fleeting** (adj.) brief, short

women's room until my bus left. I undid my ponytail and managed to twine strands of hair around my head and fit them by force beneath one of Todd's old discarded U. of Washington baseball caps. In my not-new khakis, with a kind of pale-sickly freckled skin and no makeup, I could pass for a malnourished guy, if you didn't look too closely.

I'd called Twyla before leaving home, to say I wouldn't see her in school today. Immediately Twyla picked up on something tense and excited in my voice. "What's happening, Franky?" she asked, and I said, "I'm not sure yet, Twyla. I'll call you tomorrow." I wanted to tell her more, but couldn't find the words.

I told Twyla to tell our teachers at Forrester that I was staying home today with a mild case of flu, and I'd get my homework assignments from her. Since August 27, Twyla and her mother had both been wonderful to me, calling to ask if there was anything they could do to help, but mostly there was not.

Sometimes I just wanted to scream at them, *Leave me alone!* But I knew better.

I bought a round-trip ticket to Skagit Harbor. But I had no idea when I'd be returning. I just didn't think of it at all.

While the Bellingham bus was loading just before nine-thirty-five A.M., I waited in line practically hiding my face. I kept thinking, *What if Dad knows? What if Dad finds me?* I guess I was having crazy thoughts. By the time the bus was loaded, and the door was shut, and we were chuffing along in midmorning Seattle traffic, I was so relieved I could have cried.

I had a seat by myself, pressing the side of my head against the windowpane. It was halfway true that I had flu—a sickish sensation through my body, like dread. *A special hiding place*, she'd said. I shut my eyes hoping.

"Skagit Harbor."

I was the only passenger getting off. There was no bus station in Skagit Harbor, just a coffee shop and bakery where bus tickets were sold. It seemed strange to me, and lonely, to be back here in this town I'd loved, by myself. It seemed wrong. I was restless from sitting so long on the bus. My legs yearned to run, but I didn't want to draw attention to myself.

to twine to wind **strand** (n) *Haarsträhne* **to discard** to dispose of, throw away **khakis** cotton or linen pants/trousers ranging from the very casual to haute couture **to chuff along** to make a rattling sound **dread** (n) extreme fear **to yearn** [jɜːn] to have a strong desire

Now that Labor Day was past, there were fewer people on the street. I hoped no one would recognize me.

I saw posters for the Skagit Arts Festival, which had been last weekend. I wondered if it had been a success, without Mero Okawa and Krista Connor participating.

I wasn't prepared to see the narrow white facade of the Orca Gallery with a CLOSED sign in the front door. In the display window were colorful canvases, pottery and ceramics, a glossy silk screen of wildflowers and cattails with the small initials k.c.in one corner.

Quickly I turned off Main Street and walked uphill, away from the river. The morning had begun cool and misty as usual but was becoming lighter now, the sun pale and glowing behind thin clouds. There was a smell of the Skagit River here, and a smell of wet leaves. I was feeling lonelier and lonelier. I kept thinking, *Mom is waiting for me, but where is Mom?* It was hard to shake off the conviction that she was really here, I'd hear her voice in a few minutes. I couldn't remember why I'd been so angry at her. It seemed unbelievable to me now.

But she wasn't waiting for me, I knew. No one was waiting.

No one knew where I was, in all the world.

A Freaky kind of freedom—I tried to think it was a good thing.

Then, crossing Third Street, I saw a familiar house. The pale-green house of my dream: where Garrett and his family lived.

Garrett Hillard. Hilliard? I hadn't heard the name clearly.

I wondered if he would remember me. The red-haired freckled girl he'd met a month before her mother disappeared. Before the scandal, the crime scene on Deer Point Road, the police.

I had never tried to contact Garrett, to explain or apologize. To give any reason why Samantha and I hadn't been there, at my mom's, when he'd come to take us sailing.

In that other dimension. Where it hadn't happened yet. Where Garrett came, he took us sailing. Where we were friends.

Suddenly I was walking up Deer Point Road, at the edge of town. It was like my bicycling dream; I felt breathless, my heart beating hard. I didn't want to be here really. I was afraid, anxious. But Freaky nudged me: *C'mon! No turning back.* I saw the little wood-frame houses painted such striking colors, blue, tawny yellow, lavender. And there was Mom's cabin, painted maroon. She'd been so proud of it, and of the ancient box elder looming over it. I stopped in the road and stared. It seemed so

canvas (n) (oil-) painting **glossy** shiny, bright

strange—the yellow sunflowers were still decorating the shutters and the edge of the roof. You wouldn't have known that something had happened here except there was yellow tape circling the cabin and the tree, with the continuous warning in black letters: SKAGIT CO. SHERIFF DO NOT CROSS SKAGIT CO. SHERIFF DO NOT CROSS.

The police investigation hadn't turned up much helpful evidence, beyond the obvious fact that the missing couple had departed the premises quickly.

I had no wish to slip under the yellow tape and peer into the cabin windows. I had no wish to see into that shadowy interior. *Because she isn't there. Nobody is there.* Instead, I crossed through the wildflower meadow toward the rear of the lot. I was worried again that people might be noticing me. Since August 27, residents of Deer Point Road would be quick to take note of strangers, any sort of strange behavior.

I heard a dog barking close by. I wanted to think it was Rabbit.

But no, Rabbit was gone. I knew.

Mr Rooster! There he was, preening at the peak of the old barn roof. I smiled to see him. He was more tarnished than I remembered, and askew on his perch, but handsome, impressive. Roosters are such vain, beautiful birds. I listened, and heard, or thought I heard, actual roosters crowing, from a farm on Deer Point Road. This was a farm that sold vegetables and fruit by the roadside that Mom had taken us to. I remembered hearing those roosters in the early morning, waking from sleep in the loft bed and confusing them with Mr Rooster.

Around the corner of the barn, in the midst of tall weeds, was the big sand-colored boulder, shaped like a mutant, slightly rotted pumpkin. And partly hidden by the boulder, easy to miss unless you knew what you were seeking, the burrow Mom had identified as a groundhog burrow. *A special hiding place*, she'd said. *Someone could leave a secret message for someone else in this burrow. No one would ever look here.* I knelt in a tangle of morning glory vines and reached down to grope inside the burrow. I pressed my cheek against the boulder and groped desperately for—what? My fingers found something. Paper? Plastic? I pulled it out, excited. A plastic waterproof bag, and inside it a journal with a lavender

premises (pl.) building, property **lot** (n) AE patch of ground used for building on **to preen** here: to pride or please oneself **tarnished** (adj.) discoloured, having lost external brightness **askew** (adj.) *schief* **mutant** (adj.) produced by mutation **tangle** (n) *Gewirr* **to grope** to fumble, fish

cloth cover and a purple ribbon tied around it. When I opened the bag, the sweet-spicy smell of my mother's dried flowers overwhelmed me.

TWENTY-FIVE
"they shut me up in prose"

They shut me up in Prose—
As when a little Girl
They put me in the Closet—
Because they liked me "still"—

Still! Could themself have peeped—
And seen my Brain—go round—
They might as wise have lodged a Bird
For Treason—in the Pound—

Himself has but to will
And easy as a Star
Look down upon Captivity—
And laugh—No more have I—

Emily Dickinson. 1863.

This poem! My mother had written it out in purple ink at the front of her journal. Her handwriting was beautiful as art.

The pages of the journal were made of creamcolored, finely textured paper that had a feel, when you rubbed your thumb over it, of grain. There were about eighty pages in the journal, but my mother had used only about one quarter of these. The rest were blank.

I read and reread the poem by Emily Dickinson. It was a poem I had never seen before. "They shut me up in Prose"—I felt that I understood what the poet meant, though I couldn't have explained it.

I was excited, trembling. I was scared of what I would find in this journal. But I was happy, too. I knew! My dream had led me, Freaky had led me. I felt Mom close beside me. Whatever happened now was meant to be.

closet (n) here: small side-room for storing utensils or provisions **pound** (n) <u>either:</u> prison for offenders <u>or:</u> enclosure where (wild) animals are entrapped **captivity** imprisonment **journal** here: diary **textured** *strukturiert*

Between the second and third pages of the journal, a sheet of paper had been inserted. Here, my mother's handwriting was hurried.

Francesca, dear—

If you're reading this, it means that something may have happened to me.

I hope not. I hope I am wrong. Be brave, darling.

I love you and Samantha SO MUCH.

Your mother

The first section was headed *SANTA BARBARA/APRIL 19.*

The waves! The waves of the Pacific breaking on the sand, wind and the cries of gulls. It's just sundown. God help me, I've run here to hide. My decision has been made for me. I have no choice now.

• • •

For months, years I'd known the marriage was over. But fearful of knowing. But now, this afternoon, I know.

Quietly he said, I'LL KILL YOU. BEFORE I WILL LET YOU AND THE GIRLS GO. Not a threat but a vow. Not anger but calm. This new, terrible calmness to him. When he pushed into my motel room I'd thought he would beat me, choke me, but he only shook me by the shoulders, to make me listen. Seeing me at the arts & crafts fair with the others, strangers to him but friends to me, he understood for the first time. Seeing that I had a life apart from him, that I was happy here.

IF YOU REFUSE TO BE MY WIFE, YOU GIVE ME NO CHOICE, AND IF YOU TRY TO TAKE THE GIRLS FROM ME, I'LL KILL THEM, TOO. That terrible calmness in R. I had not seen before.

His voice shook, saying, MAYBE IT WOULD BE BEST FOR ALL OF US TO DIE, KRISTA. NOT TODD BUT THE FOUR OF US. I THINK SOMETIMES LIKE NOW, YES THAT WOULD BE BEST.

The next section was YARROW HEIGHTS/MAY.

to choke sb. to prevent sb. from breathing

My weakness is I love R. even now. But I can't live with him.

His strong fingers. In my sleep I feel them.

No one would understand, R. is not mad. R. is wholly sane. Vicky doesn't understand/urges me to see a lawyer/therapist/marriage counselor. I can't tell her that I must work my way through this myself, to consult any stranger would be "betrayal"/would incur R.'s wrath.

Because Seattle is such a small city, R. says. Rumors will spread of the Piersons' marriage. He can't bear it, the public sign of failure. "Reid Pierson's wife? The second wife? Moving away from Seattle?"

• • •

Bonnie Lynn Byers. A mystery.

My husband's first wife. Whom I never knew.

So young when she died: 26.

He never speaks of her except to say she was "careless"—her death was "an accident, caused by carelessness."

Last night I sat with Francesca and Samantha and we watched Reid Pierson the sportscaster on TV. The girls adore him. They bask in pride for their famous daddy. I must protect that image of him, in their minds. I must find a way to save myself/save them. My mind beats sometimes like a butterfly trapped in a wire enclosure. The sky is beyond, but I can't get to it. My wings beat/beat/beat against the wire, desperate for a way out.

The public, he says, is waiting for Reid Pierson to fail. They loved him as a football star and they loved him injured, forced to prematurely retire. The public R. fears/loves/dreads. His TV personality. His TV smile, makeup. Hairpiece. Reid Pierson is not going to fail, he has warned me.

• • •

to incur to arouse, provoke **wrath** (n) anger, rage **to bask in sth** to enjoy sth, take pleasure **prematurely** over-hastily, too soon

I must not upset the children. They will only fear me/shun me/despise me. R. has turned Todd against me, these past few weeks. Since Santa Barbara. When I missed the family "celebration." Once, Todd loved me—what a lonely, melancholy little boy he was, having lost his mother. But now, if I touch him, he shrugs me off. If I try to talk to him, he walks away. Last night he said, Look, you're not my mother, you're my stepmother, OK?

These past few weeks the girls are starting to be aware of the tension in our household. I've seen Francesca stare at me. Her beautiful green eyes. She is so like me, at that age. I fear for her sensitivity. "Franky." Gazing at me in alarm/disgust. She seems to know what's hidden by the scarfs I wear. My long sleeves. Maybe she has overheard R.'s angry voice. I know she blames me. In her place, I would probably react like this. For she loves her father blindly, as Samantha and Todd do.

• • •

(Sometimes I feel like poor Rabbit cringing when R. storms into the room.)

Today driving Francesca home from Forrester, tried to talk to her. Asked about her swimming/diving and she lashed out at me with such bitterness I was stunned. Says she hates the name "Francesca."

R. has said "maybe" to Skagit Harbor. Our last evening together before he flew east for five days, he was more understanding/romantic. So I have hope.

The final section, the longest section, was SKAGIT HARBOR/SUMMER. Mom's handwriting here was erratic, sometimes beautiful and clear, but sometimes almost illegible, as if she'd been writing quickly, or in the dark. I couldn't bring myself to read every page, every passage. I just couldn't.

to shun sb. avoid, evade sb. **to despise** to detest, hate **to shrug sb. off** to dismiss sb. as being unimportant **sensitivity** ability to understand other people's feelings and problems **to cringe** to cower, to draw back **stunned** (adj.) too shocked to speak **erratic** (adj.) *fahrig, ungleichmäßig* **illegible** unreadable

Deer Point Road, Skagit Harbor. Work/work/work! Cleaning/scrubbing/sanding/painting! I love it.

• • •

R. calls me/expects me to call him. Which I am happy to do. On the phone we are often friends. I think R. can feel generous/forgiving in allowing me Skagit Harbor "days at a time" (his words).

Except: I miss Francesca and Samantha. So much. He won't allow me to bring them here. (Not yet.) When I call home, Francesca never seems to be there. Her cell phone is turned off. Vicky has said she can't get through either.

When I'm back in Yarrow Heights, it isn't the same. As if the girls don't trust me. Even Samantha. I know: they are frightened of their father leaving us. So much divorce/families breaking up among their classmates. I have promised R. I would never seek divorce/a legal separation/injunction. If he allows me this freedom, I can remain his wife. I hope.

Waking in the early morning. In this place where I can breathe. SO HAPPY.
(Is this selfishness? R. says yes.)
(To wish to breathe, not to suffocate? Yes!)

• • •

Such interesting/warm/generous people here in Skagit Harbor. And I have a gallery willing to exhibit some of my work: The Orca.

Working on silk screens. Slow/steady. R. has not been calling me so frequently. (I know, he's "involved" with someone in Seattle. This is fine with me. I dare not allow him to know that I know. But I wish him/them well.)

to scrub to clean by hard rubbing **to sand** to make a surface smooth by using sandpaper **days at a time** *tageweise* **injunction** order, directive

Good news: the girls will be coming to stay with me while R. is away on a shoot. R. has made me so happy, I could love him again. He laughed at me, saying that it didn't take much to make me happy, how different I am from other women.

He kissed me/framed my face in his strong fingers. YOU KNOW YOU LOVE ME, KRISTA. I'M THE FIRST MAN YOU EVER LOVED, YOU TOLD ME. AND I WILL BE THE LAST.

• • •

The girls are here! Hardly a moment to write in this journal.

Working through the mornings in such bliss. The girls are helping me with these silk screens. At last Francesca seems to be relaxed with her mother. I had worried about R. slapping her/shaking her as he'd done when she was younger sometimes/Francesca's "rebellious" personality/ but by 15 she is much more mature. I'm so relieved she has ceased being angry with me. (I even called her "Franky" a few times, and she didn't notice!) Samantha is joyous. And of course Rabbit is in seventh heaven, his favorite people feeding/petting/fussing over him and no fear of sudden loud voices/kicks.

The looks in the girls' faces, seeing their mother's work at the Orca Gallery. Of course I tried not to show it, but I almost cried. Maybe, in a small way, they can be proud of their mother, too? They don't seem to resent it that I sign my work K.C.

• • •

Such lovely/busy days/evenings. Mero took a dozen Polaroids of us at the gallery and elsewhere. How happy we appear, yes and how beautiful. Francesca's fine-boned angular face/unnerving green eyes. Samantha's soft eyes, heart-shaped face. Of course I love R., I realize. R. is the father of these girls.

Mero, my closest friend in Skagit Harbor. In all the world. Confiding

shoot (n) recording, filming **bliss** (n) joy, delight **to slap sb.** to hit sb. **angular** sharp-cornered, *kantig* **unnerving** *irritierend* **to confide in sb.** to open one's heart to sb.

in me how shaken he was by the behavior of a lover a few years ago. Mero had been depressed for a year, yes he'd "contemplated" suicide but never got around to doing anything about it. After a period of "hibernation" he resumed his life again, he lives now for work/friends/family. "Just for life itself. This is all there is."

The deep bond between Mero and me. A gay man/straight woman. Strange, and wonderful, the intense emotional connection; in ways I'm closer to Mero than to my own sister, Vicky. (Who has become impatient with me for not leaving R.) Where Vicky doesn't seem to understand, Mero does, instinctively. I haven't spoken to him about my marriage, but I know that if I did, Mero would understand immediately. Why I fell in love with R. at the age of 22, why I love R. still at almost 40, yet fear the man, and can't live with him.

R. would be angry if he knew of my friendship with Mero. He hates gays—"fags." Especially, gay athletes drive him crazy. What he'd think if he knew that the girls have met Mero ...

On the last three pages of the journal, Mom's handwriting was rushed, panicky. I could hardly bring myself to keep reading.

Sunday. July 27. Everything is changed.

R. came, took Francesca and Samantha back home with him. I'm alone now, sick/stunned. When I called the house in Yarrow Heights, the housekeeper answered saying, "Who is this please? Who is this please?" She's new, someone R. has hired. She doesn't know me, sounds vexed with me/nervous about reporting my calls to Mr Pierson....

It happened so quickly. Out of nowhere he appeared. Even the car he was driving is new. I was outside with the girls, he rushed at us shouting/grabbed a pair of pruning shears out of my hands.

We went inside the cabin to talk. The girls waited terrified in the driveway. How I wanted to shield them from this side of their father. ... I pleaded with him, tried to reason with him. He kept repeating that

hibernation here: period of suspended activity **gay** homosexual **straight** here: heterosexual **vexed** (adj.) annoyed

he had "fresh evidence" against me. Claims that I betrayed him, our agreement about the girls. I'm baffled, don't understand.

From what I gathered, it might be that he'd hired a private detective to spy on me. And this private detective has invented a "lover." To make his employer the more furious/committed to persecuting me. I think this might be it. He spoke of being "pushed too far"—being "made ashamed." When I protested, he grabbed my arm and began to shake me as if he wanted to break my neck. He shut his fingers around my throat until I began to choke, my knees buckled. Then he let me go—he laughed, saying he wasn't stupid enough to strangle me, the marks of his fingers would be on me. There are other ways, he said. He said he'd be back another time. DUMP YOUR BODY FROM DECEPTION PASS BRIDGE. IT'S A LONG WAY DOWN—NOBODY WOULD EVER FIND YOU.

He left then, with the girls. It terrifies me to think of Francesca and Samantha in the car with that man, how easily he could swerve from the highway, have a fatal "accident." I know now that it's hopeless.

Rabbit and I are huddling together in the cabin, the door locked/blinds drawn. Though I know R. is gone. I'm thinking of Deception Pass, on Whidbey Island about 50 miles west of Skagit Harbor. The summer we went there, to stay with friends of R.'s at their summer place on Skagit Bay. DUMP YOUR BODY. LONG WAY DOWN. NOBODY WOULD EVER FIND YOU.

I've been calling home. Now the answering machine is on. Maybe in the morning . . .

baffled perplexed, bewildered **to buckle** here: to bend under stress or pressure **to dump sth./sb.** to dispose of sth./sb. **Deception Pass Bridge** bridge (appr. 180 feet high and 1487 feet long) across Deception Pass, a narrow stretch of water that separates Whidbey Island from Fidalgo Island, in the northwest of Washington State **to swerve** *mit dem Auto ausscheren*

TWENTY-SIX
"now you know . . ."

Now you know what you must do.

Now you will have to remember what you've wanted to think was a dream.

It was Freaky's voice.

It was my own voice.

I called Aunt Vicky on my cell phone from Skagit Harbor. I was waiting for the two-forty-P.M. bus to Seattle. I was too restless to sit on the bench in front of the Skagit Harbor Café, where the bus picked up passengers. I'd read and reread my mother's journal and the scribbled note. *If you're reading this, it means that something may have happened to me.*

When Aunt Vicky answered, immediately she asked where I was. I told her, and she said, "Skagit Harbor! Oh, honey, why?"

I told her I'd come here to get something my mother had left for me.

"Franky, what? You went to get—what?"

A journal, I said. I was trying to speak calmly. My aunt's excitement and anxiety weren't what I needed to hear from an adult.

Since reading my mom's journal, I guess I understood that she was dead. I knew, but I wasn't thinking that, exactly. As long as I'd been reading the journal, in her handwriting, it was like she was speaking to me, and she was alive.

Aunt Vicky wanted to know more about the journal, what was in the journal, and I told her she could read it, I would give it to her to read as soon as I saw her.

And, I said, I guessed the police would want to read it, too.

"The police? Oh, honey."

For a long moment Aunt Vicky didn't speak. The understanding passed between us what this meant.

I remembered how my aunt had wanted to think my mom was alive, and would return to us. How distraught she'd been, how desperate to believe. We'd all wanted to believe.

Even my father had seemed genuine, in his "belief."

Aunt Vicky asked me again where I was, exactly, and I told her I was in front of the Skagit Harbor Café, waiting for the two-forty bus that would get me back in Seattle, downtown at the Greyhound station, at about four P.M. Aunt Vicky said she would pick me up there.

She added, hesitantly, "Franky, you should know that your father is looking for you. But he has no idea where you are."

I tasted cold. I was very frightened suddenly.

Aunt Vicky explained, "Someone on the Forrester staff called your home, and your housekeeper called your father, and he was upset to learn that you're not in school. He seemed to think you must be with me, or that I knew where you were. I assured him that I had no idea where you were, but I thought he was overreacting; you were probably just cutting classes with friends, at a mall or a movie, and you'd be back home at the usual time. He began shouting at me. I halfway wondered if I should call the police—he seemed to be threatening me. Before we hung up, he made me promise that I'd call him if I had any information about you."

"Aunt Vicky, no! You can't do that."

"Franky, of course not. I won't."

I couldn't see clearly—my eyes were blinking away tears. Every car that passed on Main Street, which had a speed limit of twenty-five miles an hour, caused me to glance up, thinking it might be my father. When a gray or silver vehicle appeared, my heart cringed.

If he finds me. If he finds this journal. If he reads this journal. If he thinks I might share this journal with anyone. If he thinks I might show it to the police . . .

"Franky? Are you still there?"

"Yes, Aunt Vicky. But I'm so scared."

"Maybe you should wait inside the café? But he has no idea you're in Skagit Harbor, honey. He wouldn't think of that."

Why wouldn't he? I would, in his place.

This was a Freaky-shrewd thought. I didn't share it with my aunt, who was already stressed enough.

She said, trying to sound calm, "Franky, the bus is due in ten minutes. There are lots of people around there, aren't there? If I thought you were in any real danger I'd drive up to get you immediately. But it would take so much longer, honey. Please—will you wait inside the café?"

Hiding from my own father! That's how desperate things had become.

I went inside the café, though. I didn't step outside again until the bus was stopped at the curb, wheezing and hissing, bound for Seattle.

***

to taste here: to feel **to cut classes** to absent oneself from school **mall** (n) shopping precinct/~centre **to cringe** to contract the muscles (here: of the heart) involuntarily **curb** (n) AE the raised edge of a road, *Bordstein* **to wheeze** to make a whistling sound **bound for Seattle** ready to go in the direction of Seattle

At the Seattle station, as the bus pulled in, I saw Aunt Vicky waiting for me. Her face was drawn, anxious. As soon as I stepped down from the bus, she hurried to me and caught me in her arms. “Oh, Franky! Your hair.” She thought I’d cut it.

We laughed together, feeling giddy. We were almost crying, as if we hadn’t seen each other in years.

The journal was in my backpack, safely zipped in. On the bus I’d been reading, rereading. I’d memorized the Emily Dickinson poem. My hands smelled of that sweet spicy scent. I had the Freaky thought that I would write in this beautiful lavender-bound journal too. I would complete the pages my mother hadn’t had time to complete.

“They shut me up in Prose.” But Prose can be freedom, too.

Aunt Vicky and I made our way through the busy terminal, moving quickly. I was safe now, I thought. (Wasn’t I? There were uniformed police on duty here.) Still I couldn’t help glancing around, thinking he might be somewhere, hidden among strangers, watching me.

Since my mother’s disappearance, Aunt Vicky had leased a small apartment in Seattle, but she didn’t think it would be wise for us to go to that apartment right now. My father had been calling her back, she said. Even Todd had called. “They seem to think you’d come to stay with me this morning, instead of going to school. They’re both very suspicious, and very irrational. Todd said, ‘You’re coercing my sister to testify against Dad, aren’t you? You’d better be careful, Aunt Vicky.’ After your father’s first call, I’d already left the apartment. I took some overnight things and booked us a room at a hotel near police headquarters.”

I was left breathless by these remarks. Aunt Vicky spoke so matter-of-factly. Franky wasn’t going back home to Yarrow Heights, it seemed. Franky, too, had *crossed over*.

TWENTY-SEVEN
the interview: september 12

When, where did I see my mother Krista Connor last?

On July 27, in Skagit Harbor. At her cabin on Deer Point Road. In the early afternoon.

drawn here: tense, worried **giddy** (adj.) here: extremely happy **to zip in** to close with a zip-fastener (*Reißverschluss*) **to coerce sb. to do** [kouˈɜːs] to force sb. to do sth. **matter-of-factly** (adv.) unemotionally

Yes. My sister Samantha and I were staying with my mother for a few days while my father was out of town.

Yes. He returned earlier than he'd planned. He drove to Skagit Harbor to take Samantha and me home.

No. He hadn't called before. He hadn't notified my mom. He just arrived. He was angry.

Yes. Very angry.

No. Not so different from other times . . . I guess.

No. He didn't touch Samantha or me. He wasn't angry at us.

Yes. They went inside the cabin. They were there for what seemed like a long time. Maybe twenty minutes.

We waited.

Yes, we were afraid.

That my father would hurt my mother, that's what I was afraid of.

Yes. Sure. I could hear his voice from inside the cabin. Maybe I heard hers. Maybe she was crying.

When they came out, my father was carrying Samantha's and my bags. Because we were leaving then.

Yes. Straight back to Yarrow Heights. To home.

Not then, but later, he said, *Your mother is in love with another man. We can never forgive her.*

Yes. I met Mero Okawa. He's a friend of my mom's at Skagit Harbor.

Mero is a wonderful person. I hope . . . he's all right.

I think probably he isn't, though.

No, my Mom and Mero Okawa were definitely not lovers. Like my father has said.

They were friends. I mean, they are friends.

If they're alive, they are friends.

Yes, I guess so. Gay. I don't categorize people, though.

Because I don't want stupid people categorizing me. It's a lazy kind of thinking, and it's cruel.

• • •

Yes. I guess I did hear them, sometimes.

Never in front of us. Mostly in their bedroom with the door shut.

to notify to inform

My father gets angry easily. I used to think my mother provoked him, but that was a wrong way of thinking, to blame my mother for being abused.

She wore scarfs, long sleeves to hide the marks. But I knew what they were.

Because I was so scared, I think. It was easier to hate her.

No. Mom never spoke of it.

She never said anything critical of him. She knew how Samantha and I loved him.

I mean, love him. I still do.

He's my father, and he's Reid Pierson. That's why.

Why? Mom was afraid, I guess. Afraid he would hurt her worse, and hurt Samantha and me. That's what she says in her journal, and I believe that's right.

If you've read the journal, then you know.

I think yes, it happened just like that.

No! I'm fine, I am not crying. I want to continue.

Yes, he did. Sometimes. It was "discipline."

I don't remember too well. It's sort of vague, like a bad dream or something you saw on TV a long time ago and have mixed up with actual life.

Spankings, when I was little. Because I would disobey, I think.

Sometimes slaps, punches, hard shakings. Daddy would grab hold of my shoulders and shake shake shake me like he wanted to break my neck.

Oh, no! I believed it was my fault. I deserved it.

I still do believe that, I guess.

It's hard to change how you feel. How you think is a lot easier.

Why? Because Dad loved us. Loves us.

He wouldn't have disciplined us, he said, if he didn't love us.

That's true even now. I can understand that. But it's a sick way of thinking, and it's wrong.

spanking (n) the act of hitting sb. (esp. a child) with an open hand on the bottom, as a punishment

I guess I would say so, yes. If I have to swear to it. . . .

Yes, my father did "abuse" me. And my sister Samantha.

(She won't speak of it, probably. She's afraid. And now that Mom is gone, she has to love Dad. I feel the same way. But I have to get beyond that feeling. I can't protect him any longer.)

• • •

When I read Mom's journal. Then I knew.

Well, I guess I always knew. But I didn't want to acknowledge it.

He said we would have to choose between them. So I'm choosing Mom.

I can't save her, I know. I accept it—she won't be coming back.

Samantha doesn't know, yet. Aunt Vicky and I will have to tell her soon.

I know, I could be wrong. Maybe Mom and Mero Okawa are alive, somewhere. Like the tabloid papers say. It's like believing in heaven—it takes away some of the pain.

The last time I spoke with my mother? August 25.

She called from Skagit Harbor. She sounded upset. She was saying she loved Samantha and me. I told her she should come back home, if that was so, but she said she couldn't, and she couldn't explain. So I became very angry at her. I was furious with her. Dad had said she was blackmailing us with her emotions, and I believed that at the time. Dad had said she had a lover, she'd betrayed us, and I believed that, too.

I told her I hated my name—"Francesca."

I told her I hated her.

Yes. That was the last time I spoke with my mother, Krista Connor.

No. I didn't hear my father leave the house on the night of August 26.

But I heard him return. At 4:38 A.M.

I hadn't been able to sleep very well. I was thinking of what I'd said to my mother, maybe. What she'd said to me.

That she missed Samantha and me. She was crying, and I know now that she was afraid of what might happen to her. She was so afraid, and I didn't listen. I hung up the phone.

I was thinking of that, and I couldn't sleep.

Samantha had come into my room around midnight. She was curled up in my bed, turned to the wall, with covers over her face. Samantha sleeps really hard sometimes, like babies do.

I'm in and out of bed most nights. I never sleep through any longer. Sometimes—it's weird—I think I've forgotten how to sleep. Some mechanism in the brain isn't working; you could "forget" how to sleep, couldn't you? I'm just lying there and my thoughts are quick and crowded and vivid like pieces of broken glass, nothing soft or dreamy about them. So I can't let go. I'm afraid.

I wasn't in bed actually. I was sitting in the dark at my computer fooling around. I'd been trying to read but couldn't concentrate. Surfing the Web, you don't need to concentrate. Almost, you don't need a brain. Your brain is the Web. You don't give yourself time to get restless or bored or even scared, just click! and you're gone.

I heard a sound outside. The wind was down, there wasn't much sound from the lake. I listened and heard what sounded like a car motor, but I couldn't see anything from my room, which doesn't face the driveway. So I went out into the hall and I watched from one of our sliding glass doors. I saw Dad's car, with the headlights off. I remember thinking, *That's strange, the headlights are off.* Because you never see a car at night driving without lights. And this car was moving very slowly, coasting into the garage. Because our driveway slopes downhill, toward the lake, you can coast, you don't need to drive. This isn't something Dad would ordinarily do, coast into the garage, but he was doing it now. And he didn't lower the garage door afterward.

It makes a noise like distant thunder. And there's a thud when it hits the concrete drive you can hear through the house.

Another strange thing: instead of entering the house through the kitchen, like Dad and Mom always do, Dad left the garage and crossed the lawn to use a door at the far end of the house that nobody ever uses.

Our house is this weird "postmodernist" house. Two stories, but because of the sloping land, parts of the top story are even with the ground. Just about every room has a door to the outside, but only two or three doors are ever used—you wouldn't have a key for every door except if you made a point to get it. So I was thinking it was strange of Dad to enter the house by that door, by the furnace room, because he'd have had to get a key for it, he wouldn't have had that key with him.

to coast *im Leerlauf bergab rollen* **to slope** *Gefälle haben* **thud** (n) a dull sound **to make a point** to make an effort **furnace room** AE room in a house where the boiler is, *Heizungsraum*

So Dad came into the house by that door, on the far side of the house. You follow the hall past the fitness room, and the indoor pool, and up some steps, and across the living room, and down some steps, and along another hall, and you're downstairs then in the hall that connects our bedrooms, and Mom and Dad's bedroom is at a corner of the hall, a big room with its own deck overlooking the lake.

I saw him. I could feel his footsteps. Actually I came close to calling out, Daddy hi! Because, if Dad saw me awake so late, he'd scold a little but in a way he'd be impressed.

Because "extreme" things impress him. Physical strain, endurance. Guts, he calls it. He hates weakness like he hates failure.

• • •

When I went back to bed it was 4:50 A.M.

My mind was so wide-awake, I couldn't not see the time.

Okay. I'm feeling better now.

I mean, I am. I just want this to get over with, please.

No. I didn't see Dad actually take the codeine tablets.

He told us a doctor had prescribed them. So he would sleep for twelve hours at least. He'd had a sinus headache, he said.

Yes. Dad's eyes did look bloodshot, I guess. His head seemed to be stuffed—he was sniffing and blowing his nose. He had trouble walking, keeping his balance. Samantha and I pretended to be his nurses, helping him walk. . . .

No. Not ever before. Not that I remember.

Yes. Mr Sheehan coached us. What to say when we were asked about Dad's medication, how powerful it was, how he'd slept through the night of August 26.

Yes. Todd, Samantha, our housekeeper, and me. We would all swear that Dad was in such a drugged condition, he could not have left the house.

And Dad, too. Dad would swear.

It's what he told police, isn't it?

Can we stop for a few minutes? I'm feeling . . . I don't feel too good.

deck (n) AE roof terrace **stuffed** (adj.) here: blocked

Yes, what I said on September 1 was not right.

I don't know if I was lying. I don't know if I was conscious of protecting my father. There was this belief in our family that everyone was against us. There was the belief that Mom had done it on purpose, that she was hiding somewhere. Mr Sheehan explained to us what we should say when we were questioned. He had Samantha and me repeat our stories to him. I was very tired— I wanted it all to be over. I would say that Dad had gone to bed around 9 P.M. and had slept for twelve hours through the night. Todd would swear to this, he would swear he'd seen Dad take the codeine tablets, I know that has been his testimony to you. I don't mean that my brother is lying under oath. I don't know what is in Todd's mind.

Did my aunt tell you that? I wish . . . she had not.

I don't want to discuss it. I'm sorry.

Like I said, I don't know what is in my brother's mind.

Yes. Because he said so.

Because he is my dad, and he said so.

Yes I believed him. Always I have believed him.

Even when I knew better . . . sometimes.

No. Dad did not threaten me. He loves me.

I did believe him, but I knew it wasn't so. I wanted to think that I hadn't seen what I had seen that night. Because it might have been a dream. I wanted to think it had been a dream.

Because Dad took my hands in his hands and swore to me that he had not hurt Mom, he had no idea what had happened to Mom, he swore!

I vow to you, honey. I love you. You know that, Franky, don't you?

So I said *Yes.*

Except now I know the truth, and I can't lie for him. I can't protect him.

I love Dad, but it's Mom who needs me. That's how I see it. The right thing to do is to tell the truth, no matter who it will help, or hurt, so I am telling the truth now.

I, Francesca Pierson, swear to this court and swear to God.

testimony evidence, sworn statement **to vow** to promise seriously

III

In The Sangre de Cristo Mountains, New Mexico: December

The Sangre de Cristo Mountains are located in northern New Mexico and southern Colorado in the United States. They are the southernmost subrange of the Rocky Mountains

The truth, the whole truth, and nothing but the truth.

It's an ideal of Freaky Green Eyes, it would never work in actual life. But in this journal, which I call the Lavender Journal, it's my ideal.

For the first twenty-three pages, the Lavender Journal is written in Krista Connor's handwriting. The remainder will be in Freaky's.

Sometimes the writing hurts. Sometimes I hate it; the words don't seem to come. And I have a miserable night, dreams of that bridge over Deception Pass . . . and the long, terrible fall into the water below.

Other days, it's easy as talking to someone you trust.

With a purple felt-tip pen I've been writing in the Lavender Journal all that I can remember. Not just my testimony, but all the rest. What happened to my mother, Krista Connor, and to our family as a result. I emphasize facts. I try not to include much emotion. Because emotions are like flames, fire. They flare up, they can cause terrible damage, but they don't last. Facts endure.

Here are facts I have recorded in the Lavender Journal:

—We are living now in the Moreno Valley of the Sangre de Cristo Mountains east of the small city of Taos and the Rio Grande River, in northeast New Mexico. (I love it here!) This isn't our permanent home exactly, though Aunt Vicky is hoping it will be, if things work out with her new job.

Aunt Vicky was awarded custody of Samantha and me by a judge for the Seattle Family Court. Since our father, Reid Pierson, was sentenced to fifty years to life with no possibility of parole, he didn't contest the ruling. No one in the Pierson family did.

"We have to get away from the Northwest for the winter." Even before the sentencing, Aunt Vicky was saying this to Samantha and me. The next week she'd quit her job in Portland and flown to Taos, New Mexico, to be interviewed for a new job, the executive directorship of the Taos Institute Foundation. "A terrific job," Aunt Vicky says, "sponsoring artists, musicians, archaeologists..." If Aunt Vicky has any regrets leaving Portland, and her family and friends there, she hasn't given a sign of it.

We're living in a hilly, sparsely populated area about fifteen miles east of Taos, in a stucco-and-adobe Spanish-style house with an orange tile roof,

felt-tip pen *Filzstift* **parole** (n) conditional release of a prisoner before he/she has completed his/her sentence, *bedingte Haftentlassung* **to contest** to oppose, object to **ruling** (n) judicial decision **sentencing** (n) statement that sb. is to have a certain punishment **sparsely** (adv.) thinly **stucco** (n) *Stuck* **adobe** unburned brick dried in the sun

an interior courtyard blooming with crimson bougainvillea, and a view of the Sangre de Cristo Mountains and the massive sky that's so unlike the sky back home, I stop and stare at it sometimes, wondering where I am. In the Lavender Journal I try to express what I feel but it sounds weak, silly. *The Southwest is a beautiful dream that doesn't depend upon the dreamer to exist.*

—After Aunt Vicky read my mother's journal, and gave it to the police, a search team was dispatched to Deception Pass, Whidbey Island, and after three days' search the bodies were found.

As the media reported, "badly decomposed and battered." As the media reported, "identification was made through dental records."

As the media reported, both Krista Connor and Mero Okawa were determined to have died by ".38caliber bullets fired at close range."

Rings had been removed from Krista Connor's fingers that would afterward be discovered, and identified by relatives, in a safety deposit box rented in a Seattle bank by Reid Pierson.

***

—Rabbit's body was never found. Only the bloodstains on my mother's quilt, which were presumed to be his.

Even after he'd pleaded guilty to murdering Krista Connor and Mero Okawa, Reid Pierson would continue to deny having hurt that "friendly little dog."

—At first, after his arrest and indictment by a grand jury, Reid Pierson pleaded not guilty to charges of kidnaping and homicide. Then, as evidence against him mounted, his attorney, Mr Sheehan, entered a plea of "not guilty by reason of temporary insanity"; when this defense crumbled, since no psychiatrist could be hired to substantiate it, Mr Sheehan tried to enter a plea of guilty to kidnaping and second-degree manslaughter, which was rejected by prosecutors. (Reid Pierson claimed that Krista

bougainvillea [ˌbu:gən'viliə] tropical climbing plant **to decompose** to decay, rot, moulder **safety deposit box** *Bankschließfach* **indictment** [in'daitmənt] the act of officially charging sb. with a crime, accusation **insanity** mental illness **to substantiate sth.** to show/prove that sth. is true **second-degree manslaughter** *Totschlag mit bedingtem Vorsatz* **prosecutor** lawyer who tries to prove in court of law that sb. is guilty of a crime

Connor and Mero Okawa had assaulted him first, and threatened to kill him, and so he'd been forced to defend himself against them by killing them; he couldn't explain why he'd forced them at gunpoint into Okawa's SUV, and forced Okawa to drive them to Whidbey Island, before killing them and pushing their bodies off the bridge.) After weeks of negotiations in the Skagit County court, the defendant decided to plead guilty to all charges in exchange for being spared the possibility of a death sentence.

—"Rat! Ratting on your own father! You'd better stay out of my way, you little bitch."

Todd hates me now. Todd will never speak to me again.

—Todd has dropped out of college. He lives somewhere in Seattle, we think.

It is my brother Todd's belief (you can check the website Todd has established on Reid Pierson) that our father was driven temporarily insane by our mother's behavior and that he isn't to blame for his actions in killing her and her "lover"; Reid Pierson should not be incarcerated in a maximum security prison in Okanogan, near the Canadian border.

Todd believes that Krista Connor's journal was a "fake" and that everything she wrote in it was "lies meant to incriminate my father," and that she and her sister Vicky "conspired to poison" me against him. Todd believes that I am a traitor to our father; he has said threatening things to me. The last time we met, in the presence of court officials, he actually lunged at me, grabbed my wrist, and shook me and shouted at me before guards pulled him off.

My brother's face, contorted with rage, hatred for me. I will never forget it.

Don't hate me. I love you.

I want to love you. . . .

You're my brother, Todd. Of our family only Samantha and you are left.

to assault sb. to hit, physically attack sb. **at gunpoint** while threatening sb. with a gun **defendant** (n) the accused man/woman **to rat sb.** (sl.) to inform against sb., betray sb. **bitch** (n) (sl. derog.) here: a cruel and unpleasant woman **to incarcerate** to imprison **fake** (n) copy of a valuable object intended to deceive people **to incriminate sb.** to accuse, denounce sb. **to conspire to do** secretely plan to do **to poison sb. against sb.** here: to stir sb. up against sb. **traitor** betrayer **to lunge at sb** [lʌndʒ] to make a sudden forward movement **wrist** (n) part of the human body where the hand joins the arm **to contort** to twist

—When Todd attacked me, I put on a pretty good show of not being afraid. I was Freaky-quick to protect myself and even managed to kick Todd (in the shin), but afterward I was shaking, and crying. Aunt Vicky and other Connor relatives were there to hug me and console me. I kept asking, "Am I a rat? For testifying against Dad?" Aunt Vicky said sternly, "No. You told the truth. You were damned brave, in my opinion. And now it's done."

—In the Lavender Journal I write *And now it's done*.
Freaky tells me that this is so, I must believe. I must try to believe.

—Samantha is in sixth grade at East Taos Elementary; I'm a junior at East Taos High. It's a fairly large school, almost one thousand students, but people are so friendly in New Mexico, it isn't anything like it would be at Forrester starting in the middle of the school year and not knowing anyone. "Hi, Franky!"—people I scarcely know are always greeting me, and smiling, and I'm made to feel welcome here, if not quite real. The way to handle a new, confusing situation is one day/one hour at a time, as Aunt Vicky advises, and that seems to work. I have to wonder if people "know" me here, but I'm not going to inquire.

I'd decided not to join any clubs or try out for any teams, just to keep to myself, focus on my schoolwork and writing, but the smell of the school pool, the quivering aqua water and the brilliant tiles beneath, made me change my mind quick. So now I'm on the East Taos High girls' swimming and diving team. In fact, I'm just about the fastest swimmer on the team, if not the best diver. The other girls respect me—I think we're going to be friends. When I was trying out for the swim coach, I overheard a girl say to another girl, "Wow! She's good."

—Sure, I miss my Seattle friends. But they're still my friends. Twyla and I e-mail each other all the time, and talk on the phone, and she's going to visit me sometime this winter. The first thing Twyla told me after my father's sentencing was that I'd done the right thing. I know Twyla meant it, because she also said she wasn't sure she'd have had the guts to do it, in my place.

to console sb. to comfort sb. **stern** (adj.) serious, unsmiling **one day/one hour at a time** day by day, hour by hour **aqua** ['ækwə] (n) light greenish blue colour **to have the guts to do** to have the courage to do

—Aunt Vicky describes herself as a "formerly fanatic" horsewoman, and here in New Mexico she's taken up riding again, and has enrolled Samantha in the children's riding school. After her first lesson, Samantha is in love. I've never seen my dreamy little sister so *determined.*

I'm into running, hiking, sometimes backpacking with new friends from school. Mostly we hike out into the foothills—this is canyon and mesa country, striated rock, hills and dry gulches and enormous boulders, stunted trees and cacti, and always the mountains in the near distance. Sometimes we drive to Chaco Park and hike among the pueblo ruins, built a thousand years ago by a long-extinct Indian tribe, the Anasazi. Always the wind is blowing here, there's shifting sunlight and shadow, a sense of spirits brushing past. There are a number of these villages, so still and peaceful you know they are sacred sites. I'm happy here: I tell myself.

But sometimes I miss Mom so much. I think of that last conversation I had with her and I want to lie down in the rocks and dirt and never get up again.

—Before we moved to Taos, Aunt Vicky drove Samantha and me up to Skagit Harbor to empty out my mother's cabin. Aunt Vicky was co-owner, in fact, but wanted to sell the cabin. "No one in our family will ever want to stay here again." We'd rented a U-Haul to carry away some of the furniture and Mom's personal possessions and artworks. Other items we gave away to neighbors and friends who'd come over to help.

It was a sad time. Melanie kept hugging Samantha and me, touching us, wiping at her eyes. Even Princess nudged at my legs, sniffing and whining. We saw that the Orca Gallery was for sale.

A tall, good-looking boy of about seventeen, with lank, sand-colored hair, came up to me and said, "Remember me, Franky? Garrett Hilliard." Garrett! I must have looked surprised, Garrett didn't look the way I re-

to enrol to register **to be into doing** to be fond of doing, like to do **mesa** a hill with a flat top and steep sides in the southwestern US **striated** (adj.) with stripes **gulch** (n) AE narrow valley with steep sides formed in the past by flowing water, but usually dry now **stunted** (adj.) not developed properly or to full size **Chaco Park** national historical park in the northwest of New Mexico established in 1907. It contains more than 300 archaeological sites that represent high points in Pueblo cultures **long-extinct** having died out a long time ago **Anasazi** a cultural group of people also called Ancient Pueblo People, or Ancestral Puebloans. **U-Haul** a North American rental company that rents trucks, trailers, and other pieces of equipment **lank** (adj.) (derog.) straight and not attractive

membered him; and the way he was staring at me, I had the impression he might not have recognized me, either, in other circumstances.

How we got through the next three or four minutes I don't know.

Garrett said he was really sorry about my mother, he'd liked her so much. . . . Then he went blank, couldn't think of what to say next. I was stammering, "I really loved being in Skagit Harbor, this is such a great place, it was the happiest summer of my life. . . ." Words so incredibly stupid and wrong, I couldn't believe what I was hearing. Freaky nudged me: *Calm down. Take a breath and hold it.* Garrett was saying, "That day I was supposed to take you and your sister sailing, when I came over, I was a little late, I saw your mom's station wagon in the driveway but nobody seemed to be around. I knocked at the door, called out who I was, looked around outside for a while, then thought maybe I had the time wrong, or you'd changed your mind and gone somewhere else, so I left and forgot about it. I mean, I didn't *forget*, but I . . . I didn't check back. And then, later . . ."

I said, "Garrett, I'm so sorry. That was the day my f-father came, and took us . . . back home with him."

My face froze, I was terrified I'd burst into tears. Garrett looked stricken, rubbing at his mouth. I felt sorry for us both!

Somehow, in spite of this clumsy exchange, Garrett and I got along really well. It just took a while. He helped us pack the U-Haul, and the Hilliards invited Aunt Vicky, Samantha, and me back to their house for an early supper, before we drove back to Seattle. Garrett and I exchanged e-mail addresses, and keep in touch. Sometimes daily. The Hilliards are planning to go skiing at Taos Valley over winter break, instead of going as usual to Aspen, so Garrett and I will see each other then.

—The last time I saw my father was in police custody. Since that time, since he's begun his incarceration at Okanogan State Prison for Men, we have not communicated.

My memory of that meeting is like a bad dream.

I was so shocked, seeing Dad: not just that Reid Pierson was wearing an ugly gunmetal-gray jumpsuit too tight for his shoulders, but something had happened to his thick chestnut hair—he was almost bald!

to go blank to be temporarily unable to understand or remember sth. **Taos valley** the leading ski resort for alpine skiing in northern New Mexico **Aspen** a ski area in the Rocky Mountains of Colorado **custody** imprisonment **incarceration** imprisonment **jumpsuit** *Overall*

I must've stood there gaping. It was one of the big surprises of my life. Looking back now, I guess there was almost something comic about my naiveté. *It was easier to believe that my father was a murderer than to realize he'd been in disguise, wearing a toupee, for years.*

Around the sides and back of Dad's head all that remained of his hair was a metallic-gray frizz, and across the crown of his head were a half dozen forlorn gray hairs. Seeing my expression, Dad touched his fingertips to his forehead and said, disgusted and embarrassed, "It's the bastards' strategy to humiliate prisoners. If I had a glass eye, they'd take it."

I remembered, in Mom's journal, the puzzling reference to a "hairpiece." Now it made sense.

Reid Pierson's famous hair was gone, and his face had lost its boyish aggression and enthusiasm. He looked tired, sulky. As if the game was over, and he'd lost. And no longer gave a damn.

Aunt Vicky hadn't wanted me to see Dad by myself. But I told her I'd be all right. Except for two guards in another part of the room, we were alone together in a windowless fluorescent-lit visitors' space, Dad on one side of a wire mesh barrier and me on the other, seated in hard vinyl chairs. During the few minutes we were together, he spoke in a rambling way, lost the thread of his words, and looked repeatedly at the wall clock. (I wondered if his next visitor was someone more important than his fifteen-year-old daughter, and even at this time I was childish enough to feel hurt.)

I said, stammering, "D-Daddy, I—I'm sorry that I—had to—"

Dad said, ironically, "Sure. I got it, Francesca."

"—because I, I really—"

I really love you. I can't believe this has happened.

I wanted to tell my father I was sorry, not that I'd told the truth to the police, but that I'd had that truth to tell, and not another; but the distinction was too subtle, I couldn't begin to articulate it, and Dad wasn't interested, in any case, in hearing it. He interrupted to say, with a smile that might have been sincere, or sarcastic, "Francesca, I don't hate you. I don't even dislike you. I forgive you." He leaned forward, smiling harder, pressing his forehead against the wire mesh, and saying in a lowered, angry voice that drew the guards' attention, "What I know is my wife and

to gape to stare **naiveté** [na:'ivte] **frizz** (n) hair that has been tightly curled **forlorn** (adj.) here: abandoned and not cared for **fluorescent-lit** *von Neonlampen erhellt* **wire mesh barrier** *Drahtgitter* **vinyl** ['vainil] of strong plastic **rambling** (adj.) long-winded, incoherent **to lose the thread** *den Faden verlieren*

that bitch sister of hers conspired to poison you against me. Poisoned a girl against her own fucking father. A girl supposed to be smart, like her father, but it turns out she's not so bright, she's putty in the hands of the cunning, so she'll have to live with that on her head, see? So I wash my hands of you—you're no daughter of mine. You can tell your precious aunt Vicky her turn is coming: my son isn't putty like my daughters."

The visit was over. Someone led me out dazed and blinking. I was too confused to cry. I would assure Aunt Vicky, who was waiting just outside, that the visit hadn't been upsetting. But I felt as if my father had grabbed me by the shoulders and shaken me until something cracked in my neck.

—SUBSCRIBE NOW! REID PIERSON DISCUSSION GROUP!

LEARN HOW YOU CAN JOIN FORCES WITH THE REID PIERSON DEFENSE FUND!

I clicked on the site just once. I have to admit it's impressive, the colorful website Todd has established, with Dad's financial support.

You can scroll through Reid Pierson's "blockbuster" career as an athlete and a TV sportscaster, which covers more than twenty years of photographs, newspaper clippings, and testimonials from fellow athletes and celebrities; you can subscribe to the Reid Pierson Discussion Group that is mostly Pierson fans, both women and men. These loyal fans believe that Reid Pierson was "framed" by authorities, or that if he'd actually committed the crimes he confessed to, there were "mitigating circumstances" like temporary insanity or self-defense. There are women who "adore" him and men who "admire" him no matter what. To these people, Reid Pierson will always be a hero. They send him donations for an appeal fund, love letters, and marriage proposals.

So far, Reid Pierson has not accepted any marriage proposal.

—A new development: the Seattle district attorney has reopened the investigation into the "accidental" death of Bonnie Lynn Byers in 1985.

—I have recorded in the Lavender Journal Dad's final words to me. *You can tell your precious aunt Vicky her turn is coming: my son isn't putty like my daughters.*

putty (n) here (fig.): wax, *Knetmasse* **the cunning** clever but dishonest and unfair people **"blockbuster"** here: very good and successful **to be framed by sb.** (inf.) to be falsely incriminated by sb. **mitigating circumstances** *mildernde Umstände* **donation** gift, (financial) contribution **appeal fund** an amount of money collected for the re-examination of a trial, *Revisionsfond*

But I haven't told Aunt Vicky yet. I wonder, should I?

• • •

—In the Spanish-style ranch house in the Moreno Valley of the Sangre de Cristo Mountains, where Krista Connor never was, her paintings, her silk screens, her weavings, her pottery are in all the rooms. In the living room with its big windows facing the mountains to the north, framed photographs of Krista Connor are arranged on a table beneath a lamp with a fringed shade. And there are the Polaroid shots Mero Okawa took of Mom, Samantha, and me: the three of us smiling so happily, Mom with her arms around Samantha's and my waists, leaning her chin against my shoulder.

Some things, you think they will go on forever.

Sometimes I come into the room and see Samantha staring at these photographs as if hypnotized and I'm afraid almost to wake her. Sometimes I lapse into this state myself and lose track of time. And I wake startled to realize that minutes have passed in my life, but no time has passed in Mom's life.

• • •

—Before we left Seattle, Aunt Vicky gave me Mom's silver ring in the shape of a dove, which I wear on the third finger of my right hand. This was one of the rings discovered in my father's safety deposit box. Aunt Vicky thought we'd have to take the ring to a jeweler to have it made smaller, to fit my finger, but it actually fits just right.

—This afternoon I went running alone. My usual route from our house is along a dry gulch that winds toward a country highway. The air was clear, cool, dry. As I ran, I tried to think of nothing except what surrounded me, what my eyes saw. In the Southwest everything is so vivid: no drifting fog, no drizzle, no overcast skies and long-lingering rain that turns people inward, brooding and melancholy. Here shafts of sunshine move across the striated outcroppings of rock and the smooth duned sand. Near the high-

fringed shade *Lampenschirm mit Fransen* **to lapse** here: to drift into **dove** (n) small white pigeon often used as a sign of peace **gulch** AE (n) deep and narrow valley formed by a river, but now dry **drizzle** (n) fine rain **overcast** cloudy **lingering** (adj.) remaining, lasting **shaft** (n) here: beam, ray **striated outcroppings of rock** (n) here: layers of rock emerging from the ground

way I heard a whimpering sound and a noise like desperate scrambling in underbrush, and there was a young dog, hardly more than a puppy, small and scrawny and covered with burrs. I stopped to pet it, and it licked my hands eagerly and thrashed its stumpy tail. It had the fox-thin face of a collie and the more solid body of a Labrador retriever, and there was no collar around its neck, no tags. "Poor dog! Poor puppy." I squatted beside it, uncertain what to do. The puppy was frantic with affection; obviously it was frightened and very hungry. If I kept running, it would try to follow me, and it wasn't in a condition to run fast. And I couldn't leave it.

I mean, how could I leave it?

I decided to check the few houses in the area, though I seemed to know, judging by the puppy's condition, that it must have been dumped by the roadside.

In the end, I brought the puppy home with me.

We haven't decided yet what to call him.

scrawny (adj.) skin-and-bones **burr** (n) *Klette, Klebkraut* **tag** (n) here: a dog's licence disc **to squat** to sit on one's heels, *sich hocken* **frantic** (adj.) hectic, wild

Additional material

1. The American Dream

The USA, a country where everything is possible?

I had come to Seattle because of a recent survey by the Centre for Economic Performance in London, on how easy or difficult it was to get rich in different parts of the world—or if not rich, at least move out of poverty.

"If you are born into poverty in the US," said one of its authors, "you are actually more likely to remain in poverty than in other countries in Europe, the Nordic countries, even Canada, which you would think would not be that different."

Possibilities

The study, together with general anti-American sentiment which has become more prevalent since the Iraq war, raised for me a question about the American dream—the idea that the United States is a place where anything is possible. I had chosen Seattle not only because Starbucks was created there, but also because Microsoft and Amazon Books and Boeing airliners all come from this small city. Dreams, if you want, which began small but are now global brands.

"Great day, isn't it?" I turned to see the lined, and drawn face of a man I will call Dave. "Are you getting what you want?"

We had met a couple of days earlier when he was having breakfast at a charity for the broke and homeless, and I had asked him if he believed in the American dream. "The American dream," Dave said, eating a muffin and wiping his lips with a paper napkin. "Well, it comes and goes. It will come again."

Winners and losers

In a low-ceilinged eating hall, maybe 100 men sat side by side along trestle tables. They had queued up since five, registered in case there was any work, then ate while security guards watched over them in case there was trouble. In Europe or just across the border in Canada, they would

prevalent (adj.) widespread **Starbucks** corporation founded in Seattle in 1971 is a very successful coffeehouse chain of today thousands of stores in about forty countries **brand** (n) trademark **trestle table** table made of long boards supported on trestles (*Böcke*)

be more likely to get social security, but this was America, where society is starkly divided into winners and losers. Strangely, though, there seemed to be little resentment or blame of government. American culture is about self-reliance and the individual fighting a way through.

"The American dream," said one of the men, his eyes dartingly alive, his nose so skewed it must have been broken many times in different fights.

"I guess you are talking about a home, wife, children and all that." "Do you have it?" I said. "No. No. I don't. I had my opportunities, but I lost."

Control

Just up the road in a small print shop, a fit, thoughtful former air force officer, Bobby Ray Forbes, was slotting calendars into envelopes. His life collapsed when his marriage went wrong. He had ended up on the street, but recently had managed to get a job and keep it.

"Oh sure, I have had the house, picket fence, two cars," he said.

"But I put myself in a position where the government could take control. Right now I am happy just being back in control. You see, what a lot of people do not know is that the key is not getting the American dream. It is holding onto it."

In Europe, the government is entwined with a lot of what we do, yet in America, I felt a sentiment that the more say the government has over you, the more you carry a sense of failure. Yet millions still yearn to come and take up the challenge. A million a year settle to start the process of becoming American citizens. Half a million actually take the oath. ... "Why do you want to live here and not in Europe?" I asked a young woman from Ethiopia, who tipped back her Seattle Mariners baseball cap and looked at me as if I were completely mad. "Europe," she said disdainfully. "What do they ever hope for in Europe? Here they have a law that you can dream to be happy."

Stark reality of the American dream
by Humphrey Hawksley, BBC News Correspondent, United States
broadcast on Thursday, 18 August, 2005 at 1100 BST on BBC Radio 4.
http://news.bbc.co.uk/1/hi/programmes/from_our_own_correspondent/4159974.stm

dartingly (lit.) moving as quickly as lightning **skewed** here: deformed, crooked **to slot** insert, put in **picket fence** AE fence made of a line of pointed sticks **to be entwined with sth.** to be closely connected with sth. in a complicated way **to yearn** to long **to take the oath** here: to promise to become a loyal American citizen **disdainful** full of contempt

2. Domestic Violence

2.1 Stop violence against women.

Beyond the protection of the law—violence in the family

"If I die, I want you to tell the world what happened to me. I don't want other women to suffer as I have suffered. I want them to be listened to."

Marìa Teresa Macias (Teresa) had good reason to fear that her husband would kill her. In the 18 months before her death, Teresa appealed to the police more than 20 times. Her husband beat and sexually assaulted her and their three children. After Teresa fled the family home, he stalked her constantly, terrorizing her and making repeated death threats. On 15 April 1996 he shot and killed her, then shot her mother twice before turning the gun on himself.

Not once in the preceding months was Teresa's husband arrested for flouting court orders that prohibited him from going near her or contacting her. Appeals to the police for assistance were ignored, rarely even documented, and no follow-up action was taken. Women's rights groups investigated the case, organized legal assistance and support for Teresa's family, and launched a national campaign.

Only after six years of legal proceedings was the Sheriff's Department in Sonoma County, California, held to account for its failure to protect Marìa Teresa Macias. Teresa's family initiated a federal civil rights lawsuit, contending that she had been denied her constitutional rights by being denied equal protection under the law because she was a woman, a victim of violence in the family and a member of an ethnic minority. In July 2000 the US Court of Appeals found that Teresa's constitutional rights to benefit from police protection in a non-discriminatory manner had been denied, reversing an earlier ruling dismissing the case. In June 2002 the Sheriff's Department paid Teresa's family one million US dollars in compensation.

The precedent-setting court ruling and award were powerful reminders to law enforcement agencies throughout the USA of their legal obligation

to assault sb. sexually to force sb. to have sex **to stalk sb.** to follow, shadow sb. **to flout** to refuse to obey **to launch** to start, set into motion **to account for** to explain **lawsuit** (n) legal action **to contend** here: to argue **Court of Appeals** a superior court that re-examines a trial imposed by a lower court **to reverse** to alter, annul **ruling** (n) decision, judgement **compensation** *Entschädigung* **to set a precedent** ['presidənt] *einen Präzedenzfall schaffen*

to protect women from violence. The ruling underlined the authorities' obligations to take effective steps to prevent and punish violence against women, whoever the perpetrator.

Yet such court rulings are not enough. According to the latest government figures, there were almost 700,000 incidents of domestic violence in the USA in 2001. Around a third of women murdered each year are killed by a current or former partner. In spite of increases in national budgets and initiatives to combat violence against women—such as "family justice" centres that will integrate support services for victims of violence in the family—women like Teresa continue to suffer because they are not given the protection they need.

from : Amnesty International Index: AMR 51/001/2004
http://web.amnesty.org/library/Index/ENGAMR510012004?open&of=
ENG-USA

2.2 The Curb in the Sky
by James Thurber

James Thurber (1894–1961) is considered to be one of the greatest American humorists. He wrote essays, sketches, fables, parables and short stories. His stock characters, first and foremost his nagging, snarling wives and their timid, happless husbands, have become classics of American literature.

When Charlie Deshler announced that he was going to marry Dorothy, someone said he would lose his mind posthaste. "No," said a wit who knew them both, "post hoc." Dorothy had begun, when quite young, to finish sentences for people. Sometimes she finished them wrongly, which annoyed the person who was speaking, and sometimes she finished them correctly, which annoyed the speaker even more.

"When William Howard Taft was," some guest in Dorothy's family home would begin.

"President!" Dorothy would pipe up. The speaker may have meant to say "President" or he might have meant to say "Young" or "Chief Justice of the Supreme Court of the United States." In any case, he would shortly put on his hat and go home. Like most parents, Dorothy's parents did

perpetrator sb. who does sth. illegal or wrong, culprit **current** (adj.) present **to combat sth.** ['kɔmbət] to fight **curb** (n) AE (BE kerb) pavement, sidewalk **posthaste** (adv.) as quickly as possible **wit** (n) a clever, or intellectual person **post hoc** immediately afterwards as a logical consequence **William Howard Taft** 27th president of the USA from 1909 to 1913 **to pipe up** (inf.) to suddenly speak

not seem to be conscious that her mannerism was a nuisance. Very likely they thought that it was cute, or even bright. It is even probable that when Dorothy's mother first said, "Come, Dorothy, eat your—" and Dorothy said, "Spinach, dear," the former telephoned Dorothy's father at the office and told him about it, and he told everybody he met that day about it – and the next day and the day after.

When Dorothy grew up she became quite pretty and so even more of a menace. Gentlemen became attracted to her and then attached to her. Emotionally she stirred them, but mentally she soon began to wear them down. Even in her late teens she began correcting their English. "Not 'was' Arthur," she would say, "'were.' 'Were prepared.' See?" Most of her admirers tolerated this habit because of their interest in her lovely person, but as time went on and her interest in them remained more instructive than sentimental, they slowly drifted away to less captious, if dumber, girls.

Charlie Deshler, however, was an impetuous man, of the sweep-them-off-their-feet persuasion, and he became engaged to Dorothy so quickly and married her in so short a time that, being deaf to the warnings of his friends, whose concern he regarded as mere jealousy, he really didn't know anything about Dorothy except that she was pretty and bright-eyed and (to him) desirable.

Dorothy as a wife came, of course, into her great flowering: she took to correcting Charlie's stories. He had traveled widely and experienced greatly and was a truly excellent raconteur. Dorothy was, during their courtship, genuinely interested in him and his stories, and since she had never shared any of the adventures he told about, she could not know when he made mistakes in time or in place or in identities. Beyond suggesting a change here and there in the number of a verb, she more or less let him alone. Charlie spoke rather good English, anyway – he knew when to say "were" and when to say "was" after "if"—and this was another reason he didn't find Dorothy out.

I didn't call on them for quite a while after they were married, because I liked Charlie and I knew I would feel low if I saw him coming out of the anesthetic of her charms and beginning to feel the first pains of reality.

mannerism here: peculiarity **nuisance** ['nju:sns] source of irritation **cute** (adj.) clever, charming **to wear sb. down** to gradually overcome, exhaust sb. **captious** (adj.) critical **dumb** (adj.) stupid **impetuous** impulsive **raconteur** [ˌrækɔn'tə:] storyteller **courtship** the period before a man and a woman marry **anesthetic** *Narkose*

When I did finally call, conditions were, of course, all that I had feared. Charlie began to tell, at dinner, about a motor trip the two had made to this town and that—I never found out for sure what towns, because Dorothy denied almost everything Charlie said. "The next day," he would say, "we got an early start and drove two hundred miles to Fairview—" "Well, " Dorothy would say, "I wouldn't call it *early*. It wasn't as early as the first day we set out, when we got up at about *seven*. And we drove a hundred and eighty miles because I remember looking at that mileage thing when we started."

"Anyway, when we got to Fairview—" Charlie would go on. But Dorothy would stop him. "Was it Fairview that day, darling?" she would ask. Dorothy often interrupted Charlie by asking him if he were right, instead of telling him that he was wrong, but it amounted to the same thing, for he would reply, "Yes, I'm sure it was Fairview," she would say: "But it wasn't, darling," and then go on with the story herself. (She called everybody that she differed from darling.)

Once or twice, when I called on them or they called on me, Dorothy would let Charlie get almost to the climax of some interesting account of a happening and then, like a tackler from behind, just throw him as he was about to cross the goal line. There is nothing in life more shocking to the nerves and to the mind than this. Some husbands will sit back amiably—almost as it seems, proudly—when their wives interrupt, and let them go on with the story, but these are beaten husbands. Charlie did not become beaten. At the end of the second year of their marriage, when you visited the Deshlers, Charlie would begin some outlandish story about a dream he had had, knowing that Dorothy could not correct him on his own dreams. They became the only life that he had that was his own.

"I thought I was running an airplane," he would say, "made out of telephone wires and pieces of old leather. I was trying to make it fly to the moon, taking off from my bedroom. About halfway up to the moon, however, a man who looked like Santa Claus, only he was dressed in the uniform of a customs officer, waved at me to stop—he was in a plane made of telephone wires, too. So I pulled over to a cloud." "'Here,' he said to me, 'you can't go to the moon, if you are the man who invented these wedding cookies.' Then he showed me a cookie in the shape of a man and woman being married, made of dough and fastened firmly to a round, crisp cookie base." So he would go on.

mileage thing *Kilometerzähler* **to amount to** to be equal to **tackler** (n) here: attacker **dough** (n) [dou] *Teig*

Any psychiatrist will tell you that at the end of the way Charlie was going lies madness in the form of monomania. You can't live in a fantastic dream world, night in and night out and then day in and day out, and remain sane. The substance began to die slowly out of Charlie's life, and he began to live entirely in shadow. And since monomania of this sort is likely to lead in the end to the reiteration of one particular story, Charlie's invention began to grow thin and he eventually took to telling, over and over again, the first dream he had ever described—the story of his curious flight toward the moon in an airplane made of telephone wires. It was extremely painful. It saddened us all.

After a month or two, Charlie finally had to be sent to an asylum. I went out of town when they took him away, but Joe Fultz, who went with him, wrote me about it. "He seemed to like it up here right away," Joe wrote. "He's calmer and his eyes look better." (Charlie had developed a wild, hunted look). "Of course, " concluded Joe, "he's finally got away from that woman."

It was a couple of weeks later that I drove up to the asylum to see Charlie. He was lying on a cot on a big screened in porch, looking wan and thin. Dorothy was sitting on a chair beside his bed, bright-eyed and eager. I was somehow surprised to see her there, having figured that Charlie had, at least, won sanctuary from his wife. He looked quite mad. He began at once to tell me the story of his trip to the moon. He got to the part where the man who looked like Santa Claus waved at him to stop. "He was in a plane made of telephone wires, too," said Charlie. "So I pulled over to the curb— "

"No. You pulled over to a *cloud*," said Dorothy. "There aren't any curbs in the sky. There *couldn't* be. You pulled over to a cloud."

Charlie sighed and turned slightly in his bed and looked at me. Dorothy looked to me too with her pretty smile.

"He always gets that story wrong," she said.

from: *The Thurber Carnival*, Penguin Books, London 1978, pp. 162—165

monomania a form of insanity in which the patient is irrational on one object only, obsession **reiteration** repetition **asylum** here: a hospital for mentally ill people **cot** (n) a small bed with high sides **screened in** (adj.) *abgeschirmt* **porch** AE verandah **wan** (adj.) pale **sanctuary** ['sæŋktjuəri] refuge, shelter

3. Man's attitude towards and treatment of animals

3.1 Animals are not ours for Entertainment.

"The idea that it is funny to see wild animals coerced into acting like clumsy humans, or thrilling to see powerful beasts reduced to cringing cowards by a whipcracking trainer is primitive and medieval. It stems from the old idea that we are superior to other species and have the right to hold dominion over them."

—Dr. Desmond Morris, anthropologist, animal behaviorist, author.

Behind the scenes, elephant trainer Tim Frisco instructs would-be trainers how to dominate elephants and make them perform circus tricks. "Sink that hook into 'em. When you hear that screaming, then you know you got their attention." An elephant trumpets in agony as Frisco's bullhook, with its sharp metal hook and spiked end, tears through her sensitive skin. Frisco, a Carson & Barnes elephant trainer, learned the trade from his father, a former trainer for Ringling Bros. and Barnum & Bailey Circus.

The fact is, animals do not naturally ride bicycles, stand on their heads, balance on balls, or jump through rings of fire. To force them to perform these confusing and physically uncomfortable tricks, trainers use whips, tight collars, muzzles, electric prods, bullhooks, and other painful tools of the trade.

We applaud trapeze artists, jugglers, clowns, tightrope walkers, and acrobats, but let's leave animals in peace. Sweden, Austria, Costa Rica, India, Finland, and Singapore have all banned or restricted the use of animals in entertainment—it's time for the U.S. to do the same.

from: Peta (People for the ethical treatment of animals)
http://www.circuses.com/

to coerce [kou'ɜːs] to pressure **to cringe** to move back or lower one's body in fear **to stem from** to have its origin in **to hold dominion over sb.** to have the power and right to rule or control sb. **behavio(u)rist** sb. who practises psychological investigation based on the study and analysis of behavio(u)r, *Verhaltensforscher* **agony** pain **Carson & Barnes** US family circus founded in 1937 **Ringling Bros. and Barnum & Bailey** the leading circus in the USA **muzzle** (n) a cover put over an animal's mouth to stop it from biting **prod** (n) a pointed instrument used to make animals move **juggler** (n) sb. who performs acrobatic acts by throwing and catching things **tightrope** a rope high above the ground used by performers in a circus

3.2 Do animals in circuses and zoos feel pleasure?

Dr. Marthe Kiley-Worthington is a renowned British behaviourist. The following text is a passage from her independent, scientific study of circus animals, in comparison with animals in zoos and in the wild. It was commissioned by the RSPCA, an organisation that has vigorously opposed the exploitation of wild animals in circuses for many years, and UFAW (Universities Federation for Animal Welfare).

To date there has been some discussion concerning the measurement of distress in animals in different types of husbandry, but little or no concern with possible behavioural measures of pleasure. That mammals at least feel something like pleasure or joy cannot be denied by any person who is prepared to admit that animals feel pain. The commonest example is of course the domestic dog which shows its pleasure at a mistress arrival or the possibility of a walk, often in no uncertain terms; the dog leaps about, wags its tail, sometimes barks, may rush backwards and forwards to the mistress, and may pant.

Whether or not the circus and zoo animals are feeling something like pleasure or joy at any time during their life that we observed, is crucial to reaching a decision concerning the ethical acceptability of zoos and circuses.

One question which is constantly asked is whether or not the animals like to perform in front of audiences. Do they derive pleasure or joy from this, in the same way as an actor might, although it might also be somewhat nerve wracking; or alternatively, do they show dislike of going into the ring and performing. How is this to be assessed in the different species?

One way of identifying pleasure on behalf of the animal is by the performance of behaviour which can, as a general rule, be associated with excitement. This is defined as: an increase in activity and often the speed of moving around, and the performance of more activities more often. In our dog example, he leaps around, rushes backwards and forwards, wags tail, may bark, or bite playfully at objects, pick up and carry objects around, show a higher postural tonus (head and tail up) and so on.

husbandry here: the care and management of animals **behavio(u)ral** concerned with behavio(u)r **mammals** animals that give birth to live babies and feed them on milk from their breasts **to pant** to breathe quickly **nerve wracking** distressful **to assess** to evaluate, judge **postural tonus** here: *Körperhaltung*

Most of the other canids show similar behaviour although the threshold at which they respond may be different. [...]

Relaxed animals, if not positively exhibiting pleasure, may be exhibiting lack of distress and fear. So animals that are relaxed in their home areas, or in company with human beings and in training sessions might be described as not distressed. This is particularly obvious in circuses where animals in all conditions, if they are under the jurisdiction of a good animal trainer, will be relaxed. It is often stated that a good horseman is one who has relaxed horses. It is possible therefore, using such criteria, to assess the attitude of the animals, and the humans to the animals by walking into any stable or farmyard. It is equally easy to see the opposite: fearful behaviour from both human stockperson and animal (lack of pleasure, and possible distress) when humans approach the animals in some circuses, zoos, stables, kennels and farms, particularly those who have policies of zero or minimal handling.

Performance

One of the main criticisms of circuses is that the animals may well dislike or even detest having to perform in front of audiences of human beings twice a day. The performances were studied, therefore, with this in mind and we walked round behind the scenes and assessed the behaviour of the animals before, during and after the performances.

One of the first criteria to consider is the behaviour in anticipation of the performance. The lights go on and the music starts, the people can usually be heard coming into the tent, and there can be little doubt that a performance is approaching. This appeared to make little difference to most of the animals. Even when they were being prepared by having their harnesses fitted (if any), or extra grooming and handling which was normal before a performance for most of the animals, they remained generally calm. We saw no reluctance to enter the ring, through the flapping tent sides, often in high winds, and usually past the very loud band in any but the least experienced animals.

Some of the big cats, particularly the younger ones, were not keen on leaping out of the cage and down the tunnel to the ring. Some of the larger

canids (n) meat-eating mammals like dogs, wolves and related animals **threshold** (n) here: the level at which sth. starts to happen **jurisdiction** control, authority **stockperson** here: someone employed to look after animals **kennels** (n. usu. pl.) an establishment where dogs are cared for in the absence of their owners **to detest** to hate, feel disgust for **harness** (n) *(Pferde)Geschirr* **grooming** (n) the process of cleaning and brushing an animal **reluctance** unwillingness

cats also wanted to leave the ring at the end of the performance. However, during the performances, most of the cats performed apparently with willingness although not always with great enthusiasm. [...]

Reaction to audiences

Many of the more experienced performing animals appeared to react positively to large and enthusiastic audiences. The act would be performed with more energy and the animals appeared to be reacting to the audiences' emotional responses to the various acts. By contrast, small audiences or unenthusiastic audiences tended to discourage the human and animal performers from making their best efforts or bothering very much at all. Whether this effect on the animals was a response directly to the audience, or to the motivation of their presenter we don't know.

Some animals had learnt that there was much audience response from doing the wrong thing, provided the audience knew it was wrong, such as the llama rolling around or jumping out of the ring, the bucking donkey bucking off its rider, or the dog knocking over its clown master. These animals apparently found the audience response reinforcing and developed the acts themselves up to a point.

from: Marthe Kiley-Worthington, *Animals in Circuses and Zoos*, Aardvard Publishing, 1990, p. 95ff

provided on condition that **bucking** (adj.) *bockend* **to buck sb. off** to throw sb. off **to knock sb. over** to run sb. down **reinforcing** (adj.) encouraging, strengthening

4. "Coming of Age" in Literature

What is an initiation story?

The name and analytic concept of the initiation story derive basically from anthropology. The most important rites of most primitive cultures center around the passage from childhood or adolescence to maturity and full membership in adult society. [...] The various critical definitions of the initiation story fall into two groups. The first group describes initiation as a passage of the young from ignorance about the external world to some vital knowledge. The second describes initiation as an important self-discovery and a resulting adjustment to life or society. But definitions within these two categories vary considerably. [...]

An initiation story may be said to show its young protagonist experiencing a significant change of knowledge about the world or himself, or a change of character, or of both, and this change must point or lead him towards an adult world. It may or may not contain some form of ritual, but it should give some evidence that the change is at least likely to have permanent effects.

Initiation stories obviously center on a variety of experiences and the initiations vary in effect. It will be useful, therefore, to divide initiations into types according to their power and effect. First, some initiations lead only to the threshold of maturity and understanding but do not definitely cross it. Such stories emphasize the shocking effect of experience, and their protagonists tend to be distinctly young. Second, some initiations take their protagonists across a threshold of maturity and understanding but leave them enmeshed in a struggle for certainty. These initiations sometimes involve self-discovery. Third, the most decisive initiations carry their protagonists firmly into maturity and understanding, or at least show them decisively embarked toward maturity. These initiations usually center on self-discovery. For convenience, I will call these types tentative, uncompleted, and decisive initiations.

coming of age the point in a young person's life at which their society considers them to be an adult **anthropology** the scientific study of the human race, its origins, developments etc. **adolescence** [ˌædouˈlesns] the time in a person's life when he/she develops from a child into an adult **threshold** (n) here: the level at which sth. starts to happen **protagonist** chief character **enmeshed** [inˈmeʃt] (adj.) involved in an unpleasant or complicated situation **to be embarked toward** to be on one's way towards

Stories of tentative initiation typically show shocking experiences which leave their protagonists distraught. Since such experiences do not always lead towards maturity, one may demand evidence of permanent effect on the protagonist before ascribing initiation to a story. [...] Among these is "Indian Camp", in which Nick Adams watches his father perform a Caesarian operation on an Indian woman and then sees that the woman's husband has killed himself to avoid witnessing her suffering. The story empasizes Nick's discovery of death, but its conclusion asserts that Nick could not believe he would ever die. If Nick's discovery is to have permanent effects, one must assume that the story's conclusion describes a protective rationalization which cannot last. If this is true, then the story shows an approach to and a temporary withdrawal from mature realization. [...] The dividing line between tentative and uncompleted initiation is, of course, impossible to establish precisely. Initiation into knowledge of sex and into sexual desire might easily fit all three categories of initiation stories, but in two well known stories such experience illustrates uncompleted initiation. In Anderson's "I Want to Know Why" a boy recognizes moral complexity in the lives of two men whose sexual behavior contrasts with their other actions and reveals a combination of good and evil. Although Anderson's protagonist remains profoundly puzzled, the depth of his concern makes it likely that he will continue to strive for understanding. More complex is the uncompleted initiation in Alberto Moravia's short novel Agostino, which portrays a boy of thirteen first learning about the nature of sexual relations, then tortured by his relationship to his young and beautiful widowed mother, and finally unable to gain admittance to a brothel, where he had hoped to destroy his oedipal vision of his mother. Agostino's desperation and seething conflicts perhaps give more assurance that he will struggle toward maturity than does the dilemma of Anderson's protagonist. [...]

distraught (adj.) worried, upset **to ascribe to** to attribute to **"Indian Camp"** a short story by Ernest Hemingway, see: http://hjem.get2net.dk/PukDegnegaard/IC.html **Nick Adams** the chief character of many of Ernest Hemingway's short stories. The Nick Adams stories are stories of initiation **Caesarian operation** [si(:)'zɛəriən] *Kaiserschnitt* **Sherwood Anderson** (1876–1941) American short-story writer and novelist whose writing had a great influence on Hemingway and Faulkner **"I Want to Know Why"** see: http://www.classicreader.com/read.php/printer.friendly/bookid.2621/sec./ **Alberto Moravia** (1907–1990) Italian journalist, short-story writer, and novelist known for his portrayals of loveless sexuality and social alienation **brothel** (n.) house of prostitution **desperation** hopelessness **seething** (adj.) here: full of

Clearly formalized primitive ritual occurs in two well known stories which portray decisive initiations: Steinbeck's "Flight" and Faulkner's "The Bear". Pepè, the young Mexican boy in "Flight", is suddenly projected into manhood when he must bear the consequences of having killed a man over a point of honor. From the story's opening Pepè's behavior shows rituals of his culture: he practices knife throwing, yearns for manhood, dons his father's garments. Perhaps more realistic is his flight from the avenging pursuer. The act itself, with foreknowledge that he is probably doomed, is ritualistic, as are his preparations, his course through the mountains, and his final deliberate confrontation of death after his case is hopeless. [...]

The greater prevalence of ritual in stories of decisive rather than tentative or uncompleted initiation is striking, but it is not too difficult to explain. The full initiations which these stories present usually grow out of strong desires for self-discovery rather than from accidents.

from: Marcus Mordecai, *"What is an Initiation Story?"* In: *Journal of Aesthetics and Art Criticism*,
Vol. 19, 1960/61, pp. 221-228

John Steinbeck (1902–1968) one of the most widely read American novelists of the 20th century, whose reputation rests mostly on his novels with proletarian themes. He received the Nobel Prize for Literature in 1962 **"Flight"** see: http://amb.cult.bg/american/4/steinbeck/flight.htm **William Faulkner** (1897–1962) famous American novelist and winner of the Nobel Prize for Literature (1949). He is regarded as one of the most influential writers of the 20th century **"The Bear"** short story discussed in: http://www.enotes.com/short-story-criticism/bear-william-faulkner **to yearn for** [jə:n] to long for **to don sth.** to put sth. on **doomed** (adj.) damned, bound to die